W9-CHW-306

Le Creuset's FRENCH ***country*** KITCHEN

Le Creuset's FRENCH *country* KITCHEN

EBURY PRESS
LONDON

First published by Ebury Press
an imprint of the Random Century Group
Random Century House
20 Vauxhall Bridge Road
London SW1V 2SA

Editor: Barbara Croxford
Photographer: Spike Powell
Home Economist: Meg Jansz
Designer: Sara Nunan at Bridgewater Design Limited

British Library Cataloguing in Publication Data
Reekie, Jennie
Le Creuset's French country kitchen.
1. Food: French dishes Recipes
I. Title
641.5944

ISBN 0–85223–828–2

Typeset in Garamond by Textype Typesetters, Cambridge
Printed and bound in Italy by New Interlitho S.p.a., Milan

Contents

Introduction

Much pretentious mumbo-jumbo is spoken and written about French cooking. In 'foodie' circles it is often elevated to the status of a sacred mystery, and reverent homage is paid to its high priests, who interpret the art to the privileged amid awe-inspiring ritual in expensive temples of gastronomy. Certainly, a meal prepared by an expert in the professional kitchen of an excellent restaurant can be a truly memorable experience. In the hands of a master, *haute cuisine* is an art, but, sadly, one that helps to perpetuate the myth that there is some special, secret skill involved in all French cooking, which the rest of us can never hope to learn. This is a pity, because the true heart of French cooking lies in the centuries-old tradition of *cuisine bourgeoise*, a tradition that advocates a simple style of cooking that is not in the least intimidating.

Good authentic French country cooking does not require elaborate presentation and exotic combinations of flavours. It is based on recipes handed down within families and among neighbours; meals prepared at home for family and friends, prepared with care from the best and freshest local produce available, following the principle encapsulated in Escoffier's maxim, *Faites simple* – Keep it simple. In other words, if you choose fresh, well-flavoured ingredients and prepare them carefully without unnecessary fuss, using the right utensils, anybody can produce delicious, authentic French dishes.

Le Creuset, who have long been famous for making real cookware for real cooks, conceived the idea for this book as a means of bringing French cooking back to the kitchen. It is an ideal combination, since there is no better material than cast-iron for cooking in the traditional French way, whether you are slow-simmering a Pot-au-feu, searing meat at a high temperature, or baking the perfect soufflé. Cast-iron spreads heat slowly and evenly, preventing hot spots where food can catch and burn; it will withstand strong heat, and yet is so efficient that most foods can be cooked at lower temperatures, helping to save energy while preserving the full flavour and nutritional value of the ingredients. This simple, versatile and practical approach is what French country cooking is all about.

In fact, the traditions of Le Creuset cookware are very similar to those of French country cooking. For many years, the same secret 'recipe' has been in use, unchanged, at the foundry at Fresnoy le Grand. Each piece is individual, made in its own mould (which is destroyed after use), and closely inspected by experienced craftsmen before it is passed for distribution – just as in cooking, where a dish may be based on a recipe hundreds of years old, but is new each time it is made, and is never exactly the same twice. One could compare the distinctive 'volcanic' orange for so long associated with Le Creuset with a classic recipe, the other colours with regional variations. However, at approximately 120 hours, it takes a lot longer to 'cook' a piece of Le Creuset than to prepare any of the recipes featured in this book.

Today's cook, of course, cannot spend days tending a stockpot over a range that is never extinguished, or scrubbing mountains of pots and pans for which our smaller kitchens do not, in any case, allow the space: today's food-lover prefers lighter, healthier meals that can be made using labour-saving devices and multi-purpose utensils. The recipes in this book are adapted to suit modern tastes and circumstances, while preserving the quality of the French country tradition, just as Le Creuset cookware is designed for the requirements of the modern kitchen. Most pieces can be used on any type of hob or in any conventional oven, and for a wide variety of purposes. A gratin dish, for instance, is as appropriate for roasts, pies and desserts as for delicious vegetable recipes and, of course, gratins themselves, while the less familiar marmitout is a lidded casserole that can also be used as a skillet or frying pan. The wide range of Le Creuset cookware allows for the fact that we may cook with gas, electricity or solid fuel, some of us on ceramic hobs; that we require dishwasher-proof handles and good non-stick surfaces, and make use of steamers and virtually fatless meat grills in the interests of health, as well as fondue and soufflé dishes in the interests of gastronomy.

The sheer variety of cooking styles that exists throughout the regions of France provides scope for using the full range of Le Creuset cookware, and *Le Creuset French Country Kitchen* offers a wealth of interesting surprises which can be cooked to perfection using the Le Creuset range. Most cooks know that Bouillabaisse is the classic fish soup of Marseilles, and that Lyons is famous for its heavily onion-flavoured cuisine, as is Normandy for its cream and Calvados. In this book you will discover less widely-known specialities, such as Garbure, the hearty vegetable soup from the South-West, or Longe d'Agneau à la Moutarde from Orleans; Périgord's delicious Crêpes aux Pommes or the Breton Moules aux Cidre, plus an unusual range of recipes for fondues, including rich chocolate and light mushroom versions as well as the better-known cheese and Bourguignonne fondues.

The great classics are here too, of course; nor would the collection be complete without some favourite recipes from Séverina, Le Creuset's housekeeper for 25 years and one of life's natural cooks, whose lunches at Fresnoy le Grand are legendary. It is her recipe for Pot-au-feu that you will find here, as well as more delicate dishes such as Tarte aux Tomates et au Basilic and Saumon aux Poireaux.

French country cooking is not *haute cuisine*. It takes less time and less money to achieve, but if anything it demands a greater 'feel' for cookery, and is truer to the philosophy of the famous gastronome Curnonsky: that ingredients should taste of what they are. As long as you do not skimp on the quality of your ingredients, take careless short cuts, use unsuitable utensils, or disobey the cooking instructions completely, *Le Creuset French Country Kitchen* will help you see through the mystique and bring French country cooking within the scope of every cook.

Bon appétit!

Soups

Soupe au Potiron

CREAM OF PUMPKIN SOUP

A delectable autumn soup with a colour to mirror that of the falling leaves.

SERVES 6

25 G (1 OZ) BUTTER

1 LEEK, TRIMMED AND CHOPPED

1 MEDIUM ONION, SKINNED AND CHOPPED

1 SMALL TURNIP, PEELED AND CHOPPED

900 G (2 LB) PUMPKIN

900 ML (1½ PINTS) CHICKEN OR VEGETABLE STOCK

1 BOUQUET GARNI

PINCH OF SUGAR

SALT AND FRESHLY MILLED BLACK PEPPER

150 ML (¼ PINT) DOUBLE CREAM

TO GARNISH: 15 ML (1 TBSP) CHOPPED FRESH CHIVES

Melt the butter in a large saucepan. Add the leek, onion and turnip, then cook gently for about 10 minutes. Peel the pumpkin, remove the seeds and cut the flesh into 2.5 cm (1 inch) cubes. Add the pumpkin to the other vegetables. Pour in the stock and add the bouquet garni. Bring to the boil, then cover and simmer gently for 40 minutes.

Remove the bouquet garni. Pureé the soup in a blender or food processor. Pour the soup back into the saucepan, then stir in the sugar, seasoning and cream. Reheat the soup gently. Taste and adjust the seasoning before serving garnished with the chives.

Garbure

HEARTY VEGETABLE SOUP

From the south-western provinces, this classic peasant soup is hearty enough to be a meal in itself.

SERVES 8

225 G (8 OZ) STREAKY BACON IN ONE PIECE

2 POTATOES, PEELED AND THINLY SLICED

2 LEEKS, TRIMMED AND CHOPPED

2 CARROTS, PEELED AND CHOPPED

225 G (8 OZ) SHELLED BROAD BEANS

225 G (8 OZ) SHELLED PEAS

10 ML (2 TSP) PAPRIKA

1 THYME SPRIG

3 GARLIC CLOVES, CRUSHED

100 G (4 OZ) GARLIC SAUSAGE, CHOPPED

1.7 LITRES (3 PINTS) CHICKEN STOCK

SALT AND FRESHLY MILLED BLACK PEPPER

450 G (1 LB) WHITE CABBAGE, SHREDDED

Cut the bacon into 1 cm (½ inch) cubes and place them in a large cocotte. Put the cocotte over a gentle heat until the fat runs from the bacon. Add the potatoes, leeks and carrots and stir lightly. Cover the cocotte and cook the vegetables gently for 5 minutes, shaking the pan frequently.

Add the broad beans, peas, paprika, thyme, garlic and garlic sausage. Pour in the stock, add a little seasoning and bring to the boil. Lower the heat, cover and simmer the soup gently for 30 minutes.

Add the cabbage and simmer the soup for a further 15 minutes. Taste the soup and adjust the seasoning before serving.

GARBURE

SOUPE AU CÉLERI-RAVE

CELERIAC SOUP WITH CHEESE CROÛTES

Celeriac undoubtedly makes one of the most superb winter soups. In the Savoie, where cheese plays an important part in cooking, the soup is frequently served topped with croûtes of toasted cheese.

SERVES 4–6

1 SMALL CELERIAC, ABOUT 350 G (12 OZ) IN WEIGHT, PEELED AND CUT INTO MATCHSTICK STRIPS

A LITTLE LEMON JUICE

50 G (2 OZ) BUTTER

1 SMALL POTATO, PEELED AND FINELY DICED

1 MEDIUM ONION, SKINNED AND FINELY CHOPPED

1 LEEK, TRIMMED AND CUT INTO MATCHSTICK STRIPS

900 ML (1½ PINTS) CHICKEN OR VEGETABLE STOCK

300 ML (½ PINT) MILK

SALT AND FRESHLY MILLED BLACK PEPPER

4–6 SLICES OF FRENCH BREAD

50–75 G (2–3 OZ) GRUYÈRE CHEESE, GRATED

Plunge the celeriac into a bowl of water with a little lemon juice added as soon as it is cut to prevent it from discolouring.

Melt the butter in a medium saucepan. Add the drained celeriac, potato, onion and leek. Cover and cook gently for about 15 minutes, shaking the saucepan several times to prevent the vegetables from sticking. Pour in the stock and milk, and add a little seasoning. Bring to the boil, then simmer the soup, covered, for 10 minutes.

Lightly toast the bread on both sides and place the slices in a gratin dish. Sprinkle the grated cheese on the bread and grill until it is just melted.

Taste the soup and adjust the seasoning, then ladle it into bowls. Float a croûte of toasted cheese in each portion of soup and serve at once.

LA SOUPE AU PISTOU

VEGETABLE SOUP WITH BASIL AND GARLIC

As in many other Niçois recipes, there is a strong Italian influence clearly evident in this soup, which is a close relation to minestrone. To make the process quicker, rather than soaking the haricot beans and cooking them yourself, use half the drained contents of a 400 g (14 oz) can.

SERVES 4–6

50 G (2 OZ) DRIED HARICOT BEANS

SALT AND FRESHLY MILLED BLACK PEPPER

30 ML (2 TBSP) OLIVE OIL

1 LARGE ONION, SKINNED AND FINELY CHOPPED

2 TOMATOES, SKINNED AND CHOPPED

1.1 LITRES (2 PINTS) BEEF OR CHICKEN STOCK

100 G (4 OZ) FRENCH BEANS, TOPPED, TAILED AND HALVED

1 COURGETTE, TRIMMED AND DICED

2 MEDIUM POTATOES, PEELED AND DICED

40 G (1½ OZ) VERMICELLI

60 ML (4 TBSP) PISTOU (SEE PAGE 127)

FRESHLY GRATED GRUYÈRE OR PARMESAN CHEESE TO SERVE

Soak the haricot beans in cold water overnight. Drain the beans and tip them into a small saucepan. Cover with fresh water, add a little salt and bring to the boil. Cover and simmer for 1¼ hours or until tender. Drain.

Heat the oil in a large saucepan. Add the onion and cook it gently for about 5 minutes. Stir in the tomatoes and cook for a further 2 minutes. Pour in the stock and bring to the boil. Add the French beans, courgette and potatoes. Cover and simmer gently for 40 minutes, then add the vermicelli and drained haricot beans and cook for a further 10 minutes. Remove the saucepan from the heat and stir the pistou into the soup. Then taste and adjust the seasoning. Serve with the cheese.

Potage Crème d'Artichauts

CREAM OF ARTICHOKE SOUP

A soup from Brittany which really should be made with fresh globe artichokes but an excellent result can also be achieved by using two 400 g (14 oz) cans of artichokes hearts instead of the fresh vegetables. Add the drained and chopped hearts to the onions, then make up the liquor from the cans with the stock to give 1.1 litres (2 pints).

SERVES 6

- 10 GLOBE ARTICHOKES
- 50 G (2 OZ) BUTTER
- 1 ONION, SKINNED AND FINELY CHOPPED
- 1.1 LITRES (2 PINTS) CHICKEN OR VEGETABLE STOCK
- SALT AND FRESHLY MILLED BLACK PEPPER
- 30 ML (2 TBSP) DOUBLE CREAM

Bring two large cocottes of salted water to the boil. Add the artichokes to the boiling water and cook for about 40 minutes, or until the leaves pull out easily. Drain the artichokes and leave them until cool enough to handle. Pick off all the artichoke leaves: these are not used in the soup but may be served cold with a dressing as a first course for another meal. Using a spoon, carefully remove the hairy 'choke' and discard, then roughly chop the artichoke hearts.

Melt half the butter in a medium saucepan. Add the onion and cook gently for about 2 minutes. Add the artichoke hearts, cover and continue to cook gently for a further 5 minutes. Pour in the stock and add a little seasoning, then bring to the boil. Cover and simmer the soup for 10 minutes. Purée the soup in a blender or a food processor. Pour the soup back into the saucepan and reheat it. Stir in the remaining butter and the cream. Stir until the butter melts, then taste and adjust the seasoning before serving.

Crème d'Haricots

BEAN AND LEEK SOUP

Haricot and flageolet beans combine with leeks to form the basis of this inexpensive, yet delicious, soup.

SERVES 6

- 100 G (4 OZ) DRIED HARICOT BEANS
- 100 G (4 OZ) DRIED FLAGEOLET BEANS
- 3 LEEKS, TRIMMED AND CHOPPED
- 2 LARGE ONIONS, SKINNED AND CHOPPED
- 1 MARJORAM SPRIG
- 1.4 LITRES (2½ PINTS) CHICKEN OR VEGETABLE STOCK
- SALT AND FRESHLY MILLED BLACK PEPPER
- 150 ML (¼ PINT) SINGLE CREAM OR CRÈME FRAÎCHE
- 30 ML (2 TBSP) CHOPPED FRESH CHIVES

Soak the haricot and flageolet beans overnight in cold water. Drain the beans and put them into a medium saucepan with the leeks, onions, marjoram and stock. Bring to the boil, cover and simmer gently for 1½–2 hours or until the beans can be crushed easily. Purée the soup in a blender or food processor, then pour it back into the pan. Add seasoning and reheat the soup without boiling. Just before serving stir in the cream and heat gently for a minute or so. Do not boil the soup. Taste the soup and adjust the seasoning, then serve sprinkled with the chives.

Crème de Coquillages

CREAM OF SHELLFISH SOUP

In Brittany, where this recipe originates, a wide variety of shellfish are used, including scallops, oysters, mussels, whelks and cockles; however you may use any mixture you prefer. Cooked prawns or shrimps can also be used: peel them and add the shells to the water used for cooking the fish.

SERVES 6

900 G (2 LB) MIXED SHELLFISH (SEE ABOVE)

2 TARRAGON SPRIGS

1 ONION, SKINNED AND CHOPPED

2 CELERY STICKS, CHOPPED

25 G (1 OZ) BUTTER

25 G (1 OZ) PLAIN FLOUR

300 ML (½ PINT) DRY WHITE WINE

150 ML (¼ PINT) DOUBLE CREAM

2 EGG YOLKS

30 ML (2 TBSP) CHOPPED FRESH PARSLEY

SALT AND FRESHLY MILLED BLACK PEPPER

Prepare the shellfish according to their type. Set aside any seafood which is already removed from the shell, for example scallops or oysters. Save the liquor from oysters to add to the soup. Thoroughly scrub all the cockle and mussel shells, discarding any that are open and which do not close when tapped firmly. Put them into a large saucepan with 600 ml (1 pint) water, the tarragon, onion and celery. Cover and bring to the boil. Simmer gently for about 10 minutes or until all the shells open. Add any shelled, uncooked shellfish, such as scallops and oysters, and leave the pan off the heat for a further 10 minutes – the heat of the liquor in the pan will cook the raw shellfish. Strain the shellfish and reserve the cooking liquor. Remove all the shellfish from the shells and discard any unopened shells. Cut up any large shellfish, such as scallops. Set all the shellfish aside.

Melt the butter in a medium saucepan. Add the flour and cook, stirring for 1 minute. Remove the pan from the heat and gradually stir in the wine. Replace the saucepan on the heat and bring the soup to the boil, stirring all the time. Gradually stir in the reserved cooking liquor and simmer gently for 5 minutes.

Stir the cream into the egg yolks, then add the mixture to the soup with the reserved shellfish and the parsley. Heat gently, stirring, for a few minutes without boiling, then taste and adjust the seasoning before serving the soup.

Bisque de Crabe

CRAB BISQUE

This recipe may also be used for lobster or large cooked prawns.

SERVES 6

1 COOKED CRAB, ABOUT 1.4 KG (3 LB) IN WEIGHT

750 ML (1¼ PINTS) WATER

300 ML (½ PINT) DRY WHITE WINE, SUCH AS A MUSCADET

PARED RIND OF 1 LEMON

JUICE OF ½ LEMON

1 ONION, SKINNED AND QUARTERED

1 CELERY STICK, CHOPPED

SALT

6 PEPPERCORNS

1 BOUQUET GARNI

2 LARGE DILL SPRIGS

300 ML (½ PINT) SINGLE CREAM

2 EGG YOLKS

TO GARNISH: DILL OR PARSLEY SPRIGS

Remove all the meat from the crab and pound it in a mortar or finely chop in a blender or food processor. Thoroughly scrub the shell and put it into a large saucepan with the remains of the claws, the water, wine, lemon rind and juice, onion, celery, salt, peppercorns, bouquet garni and dill. Bring slowly to the boil, cover and simmer gently for 30 minutes. Strain the stock into a medium saucepan. Blend the cream with the egg yolks and stir in about 150 ml (¼ pint) of the hot stock. Pour the egg and cream mixture into the soup. Stir in the crab meat and heat gently without boiling. Taste and adjust the seasoning before serving, garnished with dill.

Soupe aux Tomates et à l'Estragon

TOMATO AND TARRAGON SOUP

An excellent chilled soup for casual summer lunch parties and picnics.

SERVES 4–6

30 ML (2 TBSP) VIRGIN OLIVE OIL

1 MEDIUM ONION, SKINNED AND CHOPPED

1 GARLIC CLOVE, CRUSHED

1 MEDIUM POTATO, PEELED AND SLICED

675 G (1½ LB) RIPE TOMATOES, SKINNED AND CHOPPED

15 ML (1 TBSP) CHOPPED FRESH TARRAGON

300 ML (½ PINT) CHICKEN STOCK

SALT AND FRESHLY MILLED BLACK PEPPER

GRATED RIND AND JUICE OF ½ ORANGE

PINCH OF SUGAR (OPTIONAL)

Heat the oil in a medium saucepan. Add the onion, garlic and potato and cook gently for 5 minutes. Stir in the tomatoes and tarragon, making sure all the vegetables are well mixed, then pour in the stock. Add a little seasoning, cover and simmer gently for 20 minutes. Purée the soup in a blender or food processor. Stir in the orange rind and juice, then taste and adjust the seasoning, adding the sugar if necessary. Chill the soup thoroughly before serving.

Bouillabaisse
MIXED FISH SOUP

Saffron is used in this hearty fish soup to enhance both the colour and flavour.

SERVES 6

- 1.8 KG (4 LB) FILLETS OF MIXED WHITE FISH AND SHELLFISH, SUCH AS WHITING, CONGER EEL, MONKFISH, AND COOKED LANGOUSTINES OR MUSSELS, CLEANED (SEE PAGE 57)
- 150 ML (¼ PINT) OLIVE OIL
- 2–3 ONIONS, SKINNED AND SLICED
- 1 LEEK, TRIMMED AND THINLY SLICED
- PARED RIND OF ½ ORANGE
- 3 GARLIC CLOVES, CRUSHED
- 1 BAY LEAF
- FEW PARSLEY SPRIGS
- SALT AND FRESHLY MILLED BLACK PEPPER
- PINCH OF SAFFRON STRANDS
- 450 G (1 LB) TOMATOES, SKINNED AND SLICED

Wash the fish and pat dry with absorbent kitchen paper. Remove any skin, then cut fish into fairly large, thick pieces.

Heat the oil in a large casserole and gently fry the onions and leek for 5 minutes or until soft. Finely shred the orange rind, then stir into the onion and leek with the garlic, herbs and seasoning. Dissolve the saffron in a little hot water.

Add the fish with the tomatoes. Stir in the saffron water and just enough cold water to cover. Bring to the boil and simmer, uncovered, for 8 minutes. Add the langoustines or mussels and cook for a further 5–8 minutes. Using a slotted spoon, quickly remove the fish and arrange in a serving dish. Leave the langoustines or mussels in their shells. Strain the soup and season, then pour into the dish. Serve immediately with Rouille (see page 128).

Soupe à l'Oignon
ONION SOUP

This famous soup is very sustaining, partly due to the toasted slices of French bread with cheese that accompany it.

SERVES 4

- 50 G (2 OZ) BUTTER
- 15 ML (1 TBSP) VEGETABLE OIL
- 450 G (1 LB) ONIONS, SKINNED AND FINELY SLICED
- 2.5 ML (½ TSP) SUGAR
- SALT AND FRESHLY MILLED BLACK PEPPER
- 15 ML (1 TBSP) PLAIN FLOUR
- 1 LITRE (1¾ PINTS) BEEF STOCK
- 150 ML (¼ PINT) DRY WHITE WINE
- 75 G (3 OZ) GRUYÈRE CHEESE, GRATED
- 4 SLICES OF FRENCH BREAD, TOASTED ON BOTH SIDES
- 45 ML (3 TBSP) COGNAC

Melt the butter with the oil in a large saucepan. Add the onions, stir well, cover and cook gently, stirring occasionally, for 20 minutes. When the onions are completely soft, add the sugar and a pinch of salt and increase the heat to high. Cook for about 2 minutes until the onions caramelise slightly. Stir in the flour and cook for 1 minute until light brown. Pour in the stock and wine, add pepper to taste and bring to the boil. Lower the heat, partially cover and simmer for 40 minutes.

Pile a little grated Gruyère on to each round of toasted bread and brown lightly under the grill.

Add the Cognac to the soup. Stir well, then taste and adjust the seasoning. Pour into heated soup bowls and float the toasted bread on top. Serve immediately.

Hors D'oeuvres and Egg Dishes

Tarte à la Tomate et au Basilic

FRESH TOMATO AND BASIL TART

Well-flavoured tomatoes are essential to this simple country dish.

SERVES 8

1 QUANTITY PÂTE BRISÉE (SEE PAGE 156)

30 ML (2 TBSP) FINELY SHREDDED FRESH BASIL

675 G (1½ LB) FIRM TOMATOES, SKINNED AND THICKLY SLICED

SALT AND FRESHLY MILLED BLACK PEPPER

60 ML (4 TBSP) OLIVE OIL

Roll out the pastry and use it to line a 26 cm (10¼ inch) flan dish. Prick the base lightly. Place a sheet of greaseproof paper in the pastry case and top with dried peas or baking beans. Bake at 200°C (400°F) mark 6 for 10 minutes. Remove the greaseproof paper and beans, and bake for a further 5 minutes to dry out the base. Reduce the oven temperature to 180°C (350°F) mark 4. Sprinkle half the basil over the pastry base. Add the sliced tomatoes, arranging them evenly on the pastry. Season generously with black pepper but adding only a little salt. Spoon the olive oil over the tomatoes and sprinkle the remaining basil on top. Bake the tart for 15–20 minutes or until the tomatoes are just cooked. Serve either hot or cold.

Note: To skin tomatoes, plunge them into freshly boiling water and leave them for 1 minute. Drain and place in cold water for 1 minute, then slit the skins and slide them off.

Pipérade

EGGS WITH PEPPER AND TOMATOES

One of the most renowned French regional dishes, this speciality of the Basque is delicious eaten hot or cold.

SERVES 4

45 ML (3 TBSP) OLIVE OIL

1 ONION, SKINNED AND FINELY CHOPPED

2 GARLIC CLOVES, CRUSHED

4 RED PEPPERS, SEEDED AND CUT INTO 1 CM (½ INCH) SQUARES

450 G (1 LB) TOMATOES, SKINNED, QUARTERED AND SEEDED

8 EGGS

SALT AND FRESHLY MILLED BLACK PEPPER

4 SLICES OF BAYONNE HAM

Heat the oil in a medium-sized saucepan. Add the onion, garlic and peppers and cook, stirring occasionally, for about 5 minutes. Lightly mix in the tomatoes and continue cooking for a further 10 minutes. Meanwhile, beat the eggs with seasoning. Pour the eggs into the pan and cook gently over a low heat, stirring all the time, until the eggs are creamy. The pipérade may be served immediately or allowed to cool before serving. To serve, place a slice of ham on each of four plates and divide the pipérade between them.

TARTE À LA TOMATE ET AU BASILIC

Omelette aux Fines Herbes

FRESH HERB OMELETTE

A simple, classical omelette which has no equal.

SERVES 1

- 2 EGGS
- 10 ML (2 TSP) WATER
- SALT AND FRESHLY MILLED BLACK PEPPER
- 10 ML (2 TSP) CHOPPED FRESH PARSLEY
- 5 ML (1 TSP) CHOPPED FRESH CHIVES
- 5 ML (1 TSP) CHOPPED FRESH CHERVIL
- PINCH OF CHOPPED FRESH TARRAGON
- 15 G (½ OZ) BUTTER

Put a serving plate to warm. Lightly beat the eggs with the water and seasoning, then add the herbs. Heat the butter in a 20 cm (8 inch) omelette pan until it is foaming. Pour in the egg mixture all at once. Tip the pan and stir the eggs lightly with a fork, pushing the cooked edges into the centre.

When the underside of the omelette is golden brown and the top still moist and creamy, loosen the edges with a palette knife. Tip the pan away from you, giving it a firm jerk so that the omelette flips slightly and folds in half. Slide the omelette on to the heated plate and serve immediately.

Omelette Provençale

An excellent way of using up a few spoonfuls of ratatouille you may have left in the refrigerator. Served with a glass of red wine and a chunk of crisp, country bread, it is a true gourmet's delight.

SERVES 2

- 60 ML (4 TBSP) RATATOUILLE (SEE PAGE 116)
- 4 EGGS
- 15 ML (1 TBSP) WATER
- SALT AND FRESHLY MILLED BLACK PEPPER
- 15 G (½ OZ) BUTTER

Put a serving plate to warm. Heat the ratatouille in a small saucepan. Beat the eggs with the water and seasoning. Melt the butter in a large omelette pan until it is foaming. Pour in the egg mixture all at once. Tip the pan and stir the eggs lightly with a fork, pushing the cooked edges into the centre of the omelette.

When the underside of the omelette is golden brown and the top still moist and creamy, loosen the edges with a palette knife. Spoon the ratatouille over half of the omelette and fold the other half over to enclose the ratatouille. Slide the omelette out on to the heated serving plate and serve at once.

Soufflé au Fromage et aux Herbes

CHEESE AND HERB SOUFFLÉ

Care should be taken when whisking the egg whites not to over-whisk.

SERVES 8 AS A STARTER, 4–6 AS A MAIN COURSE

50 G (2 OZ) BUTTER PLUS EXTRA FOR GREASING

50 G (2 OZ) PLAIN FLOUR

300 ML (½ PINT) MILK

175 G (6 OZ) GRUYÈRE CHEESE, GRATED

50 G (2 OZ) PARMESAN CHEESE, GRATED

8 EGGS, SEPARATED

SALT AND FRESHLY MILLED BLACK PEPPER

5 ML (1 TSP) DIJON FRENCH MUSTARD

22.5 ML (1½ TBSP) CHOPPED FRESH PARSLEY

22.5 ML (1½ TBSP) CHOPPED FRESH CHERVIL

22.5 ML (1½ TBSP) CHOPPED FRESH CHIVES

Thoroughly butter a 2.5 litre (4¼ pint) soufflé dish. Melt the butter in a large saucepan. Add the flour and cook, stirring, for 1 minute. Gradually pour in the milk, stirring all the time, and bring to the boil to make a thick, smooth sauce. Remove the saucepan from the heat and stir in both types of cheese. Beat in the egg yolks, one at a time, the seasoning, mustard and herbs.

Whisk the egg whites until they form soft peaks: they should not be too stiff and dry or they will be too difficult to fold in but you should be able to turn the bowl upside down without dropping the egg out. Beat one small spoonful of the whites into the cheese mixture, then carefully fold in the remaining whites. Turn the soufflé mixture into the prepared dish. Bake at 160°C (325°F) mark 3 for 1 hour or until the soufflé is well risen and golden brown. Serve at once. (If the soufflé is baked in a fan-assisted oven, it will be cooked after about 45 minutes.)

Tarte à l'Oignon

ONION TART

A classic French dish which demands good quality, large onions. If they are organic so much the better – onions which are grown without the use of chemical fertilisers contain less water.

SERVES 8

1 QUANTITY PÂTE BRISÉE (SEE PAGE 156)

75 G (3 OZ) BUTTER

1.4 KG (3 LB) ONIONS, SKINNED AND THINLY SLICED

6 EGGS

300 ML (½ PINT) DOUBLE CREAM

SALT AND FRESHLY MILLED BLACK PEPPER

GOOD 1.25 ML (¼ TSP) GRATED NUTMEG

Roll out the pastry and use to line a 26 cm (10¼ inch) flan dish. Roll the rolling pin over the top of the dish to trim the edges of the pastry, then chill the flan case while preparing the filling.

Melt the butter in a large frying pan. Add the onions and cook gently for about 40 minutes, or until soft and golden. Turn and stir the onions several times as they cook so that they brown evenly.

Beat the eggs with the cream, plenty of seasoning and the nutmeg. Add the onions to the egg mixture and stir well. Spoon this filling into the prepared pastry case. Bake at 200°C (400°F) mark 6 for 20 minutes. Reduce the oven temperature to 160°C (325°F) mark 3 and continue cooking for a further 15–20 minutes, until the filling is set and lightly browned. Serve freshly baked or allow the tart to cool before serving.

Oeufs en Cocotte aux Crevettes

BAKED EGGS WITH PRAWNS AND FRESH DILL

An excellent starter or light luncheon dish served with a salad.

SERVES 4

15 G (½ OZ) BUTTER FOR GREASING

100 G (4 OZ) PEELED COOKED PRAWNS

15 ML (1 TBSP) CHOPPED FRESH DILL

SALT AND FRESHLY MILLED BLACK PEPPER

60 ML (4 TBSP) DOUBLE CREAM

4 EGGS

Lightly butter four individual ramekin or cocotte dishes and divide the prawns and dill between them. Season the prawns with pepper and pour 15 ml (1 tbsp) of cream into each dish. Pour hot water into a medium gratin dish to a depth of about 2.5 cm (1 inch). Stand the ramekins or cocottes in this bain marie. Bake at 180°C (350°F) mark 4 for 10 minutes.

Carefully break an egg into each dish, season them lightly and cover each dish with foil. Bake for about a further 10 minutes or until the egg whites are just set and the yolks are still soft. Serve immediately.

Salade aux Fruits de Mer Chaude

WARM SEAFOOD SALAD

Tarragon is used to flavour the dressing for this seafood salad starter.

SERVES 4

450 G (1 LB) MUSSELS

450 G (1 LB) PRAWNS IN THEIR SHELLS

225 G (8 OZ) COD FILLET

600 ML (1 PINT) COURT BOUILLON

DRESSING

45 ML (3 TBSP) OLIVE OIL

15 ML (1 TBSP) TARRAGON VINEGAR

5 ML (1 TSP) COARSE GROUND MUSTARD

10 ML (2 TSP) CHOPPED FRESH TARRAGON

SALT AND FRESHLY MILLED BLACK PEPPER

1 CURLY ENDIVE, SHREDDED

Wash and scrub the mussels well, discarding any that are open, and remove the beards (see page 57). Put into a large saucepan with the prawns and cod. Add the court bouillon, cover and cook for about 10 minutes or until the mussel shells open. Carefully strain off the liquid. Take the mussels out of their shells, skin and flake the cod, and peel the prawns. Return the fish to the saucepan to keep warm. While the fish is cooking, mix together all the dressing ingredients. Have ready four serving plates with a little endive on each. Carefully toss the warm fish in the dressing. Pile a little of the mixture on to each plate. Serve immediately.

SALADE AUX FRUITS DE MER CHAUDE

Tarte aux Langoustines

FRESH PRAWN TART

A sensational starter for a dinner party, this tart made with large green prawns tastes even better than it looks.

SERVES 8

1 QUANTITY PÂTE BRISÉE (SEE PAGE 156)

450 G (1 LB) LARGE GREEN PRAWNS OR SCAMPI TAILS

75 G (3 OZ) BUTTER

2 BUNCHES SPRING ONIONS, TRIMMED AND FINELY CHOPPED

100 G (4 OZ) OYSTER MUSHROOMS

6 EGGS

600 ML (1 PINT) SINGLE CREAM OR CRÈME FRAÎCHE

SALT AND FRESHLY MILLED BLACK PEPPER

2.5 ML (½ TSP) GRATED NUTMEG

Roll out the pastry and use it to line a 26 cm (10¼ inch) flan dish. Prick the base lightly with a fork and place a sheet of greaseproof paper in the pastry case. Fill with baking or dried beans and bake at 200°C (400°F) mark 6 for 10 minutes. Remove the greaseproof paper and beans, then bake the pastry case for a further 5 minutes to dry out the base.

Peel the shellfish while the pastry is cooking. Slit each one in half down the back and carefully lift out the black vein. Melt the butter in a small saucepan. Add the onions and cook them gently for 2–3 minutes. Use a draining spoon to remove the onions from the saucepan and put them on one side. Increase the heat, add the shellfish to the butter remaining in the pan and fry them for 2–3 minutes or until they are just cooked. Do not, on any account, overcook the shellfish or they will be tough. Use a draining spoon to lift the shellfish from the pan and set them aside. Add the mushrooms to the pan and cook them gently for 5 minutes. Take the pan off the heat.

Beat the eggs, then beat in the cream, seasoning and nutmeg. Stir in the onions and mushrooms, together with the liquor from the pan. Scatter the shellfish evenly in the pastry case, then ladle the cream mixture over them. Bake the tart for 10 minutes, then reduce the oven temperature to 160°C (325°F) mark 3 and cook for a further 30 minutes or until the filling is just set. Do not overcook the tart or the shellfish will toughen.

Poireaux Vinaigrette

LEEKS IN FRENCH DRESSING

The flavour of walnut or hazelnut oil combines well with cooked leeks to make a delicious starter.

SERVES 4

8 YOUNG LEEKS, TRIMMED

SALT

60 ML (4 TBSP) SAUCE VINAIGRETTE (SEE PAGE 128), MADE WITH HAZELNUT OR WALNUT OIL

30 ML (2 TBSP) CHOPPED FRESH PARSLEY

The leeks must be thoroughly cleaned; if using medium vegetables, cut them in half lengthways. Quarter fill a large saucepan with water, add a little salt and bring to the boil. Add the leeks, cover and cook for about 10–15 minutes or until they are just tender. Drain the leeks and leave them in a colander for about 5 minutes, or until all the water has drained out of them.

Arrange the leeks in a serving dish, pour the vinaigrette over them and sprinkle with the parsley. Leave to marinate for about 2 hours before serving.

Crottins de Chèvre

GRILLED GOAT'S CHEESE

This dish can be served either as a starter or as a savoury after the main course.

SERVES 4 OR 8

- 1 GARLIC CLOVE, HALVED
- 8 THIN SLICES OF FRENCH BREAD FROM A BAGUETTE
- 45 ML (3 TBSP) EXTRA VIRGIN OLIVE OIL
- 1 HEAD OF CHICORY, TRIMMED
- A FEW LEAVES OF LAMB'S LETTUCE
- SALT AND FRESHLY MILLED BLACK PEPPER
- 175 G (6 OZ) GOAT'S CHEESE, OR 4 INDIVIDUAL 'CROTTINS'

Rub the garlic clove all over one side of each slice of the bread, then lay the slices in a large oval gratin dish. Sprinkle with 15 ml (1 tbsp) of the oil and cook at 110°C (225°F) mark ¼ for about 45 minutes or until crisp.

Divide the endive between four small plates and add the lamb's lettuce. Season and sprinkle with the remaining oil. Remove the rind from the cheese and mash it lightly with a fork. Spread the mashed cheese over the toasts, right out to the edge of the bread. If using 'crottins', slice them horizontally and place half on each piece of toast. Put the cheese under a moderately hot grill for 3-4 minutes or until it is bubbling. Place two cheese toasts on each plate of salad and serve at once.

Salade de Piments et Fenouils

RED PEPPER AND FENNEL SALAD

Serve this salad either as a starter on its own or with two or three other salads for a main course.

SERVES 4–6

- 45 ML (3 TBSP) OLIVE OIL
- 1 MEDIUM ONION, SKINNED AND FINELY CHOPPED
- 1 GARLIC CLOVE, CRUSHED
- 4 RED PEPPERS, SEEDED AND SLICED INTO RINGS
- SALT AND FRESHLY MILLED BLACK PEPPER
- 2 SMALL BULBS FENNEL, QUARTERED LENGTHWAYS

Heat the oil in a large saucepan. Add the onion and garlic, and cook gently for about 5 minutes. Add the peppers and stir them with the onion. Stir in seasoning. Arrange the pieces of fennel in the pan, pushing them well down into the other vegetables. Add 30 ml (2 tbsp) water. Cover and cook gently for 30 minutes, or until the fennel is tender. Cool before serving.

SALADE MÉLANGÉE

MIXED LEAF SALAD

Croûtons make an excellent addition to this salad. Add crushed garlic when frying the cubes of bread.

SERVES 4–6

2 HEADS OF RADICCHIO

1 HEAD OF CURLY ENDIVE

SEVERAL LEAVES OF ROCKET

FRESH SPINACH LEAVES

FEW NASTURTIUM LEAVES

CHOPPED FRESH HERBS, SUCH AS CHIVES, PARSLEY, CHERVIL

5 ML (1 TSP) WHOLEGRAIN MUSTARD

2.5 ML (½ TSP) SUGAR

1 GARLIC CLOVE, CRUSHED

15 ML (1 TBSP) WHITE WINE VINEGAR

30 ML (2 TBSP) OLIVE OIL

SALT AND FRESHLY MILLED BLACK PEPPER

Tear all the salad leaves into pieces approximately the same size, and mix together in a bowl with the herbs.

Combine the mustard, sugar, garlic, vinegar and oil in a screw-topped jar and shake well. Season to taste.

Just before serving, shake the dressing again and pour over the salad. Toss well.

Left SALADE DE PIMENTS ET FENOUILS *(see page 29), Centre* CROTTINS DE CHÈVRE *(see page 29), Right* SALADE MÉLANGÉE *(above)*

Salade de Moules

MUSSEL SALAD

Whilst one could use ready-cooked mussels for this dish, they can never compare with the flavour of plump mussels that have been freshly cooked at home.

SERVES 8

3.4 LITRES (6 PINTS) MUSSELS
4 SHALLOTS, SKINNED AND CHOPPED
A FEW PARSLEY STALKS
2 THYME SPRIGS
BAY LEAF
A FEW BLACK PEPPERCORNS
60 ML (4 TBSP) VIRGIN OLIVE OIL
30 ML (2 TBSP) LEMON JUICE
15 ML (1 TBSP) CHOPPED FRESH PARSLEY
30 ML (2 TBSP) CHOPPED FRESH CHERVIL
SALT AND FRESHLY MILLED BLACK PEPPER

TO GARNISH: LEMON WEDGES

Clean and prepare the mussels as for Moules au gratin (page 57). Put the shallots, parsley stalks, thyme, bay leaf, peppercorns and 300 ml (½ pint) water into a very large saucepan and bring to the boil. Cover and simmer for 5 minutes. Add the mussels, cover, increase the heat and cook quickly, shaking the pan constantly. As soon as the mussels are all open, remove the pan from the heat.

When the mussels are just cool enough to handle take them out of their shells and place in a bowl. Discard any shells that have not opened. Whisk the oil with the lemon juice and pour this dressing over the mussels while they are still warm. Toss the mussels lightly in the dressing, then sprinkle the herbs over and leave to cool. Taste and adjust the seasoning, before turning the mussels into a serving dish. Garnish the salad with lemon wedges.

Salade Tiède aux Lardons

WARM SALAD WITH BACON

The original warm salad consisted of lardons – strips of pork fat taken from the belly – browned and tossed with lettuce, endive and/or young dandelion leaves. Strips of streaky bacon replace the lardons in this recipe.

SERVES 4

½ ENDIVE
1 SMALL HEAD OF RADICCHIO
25 G (1 OZ) LAMB'S LETTUCE OR DANDELION LEAVES
225 G (8 OZ) STREAKY BACON, PREFERABLY IN ONE PIECE, CUT INTO 2.5 CM (1 INCH) STRIPS (SEE METHOD)
45 ML (3 TBSP) WALNUT OIL
15 ML (1 TBSP) COGNAC VINEGAR OR RED WINE VINEGAR
2.5 ML (½ TSP) MILD WHOLEGRAIN MUSTARD
SALT AND FRESHLY MILLED BLACK PEPPER

Wash and dry the salad ingredients and break the endive into small pieces. Divide the endive, radicchio leaves and lamb's lettuce or dandelion leaves between four plates.

The bacon strips should be about 0.5 cm (¼ inch) thick. Put the strips in a small frying pan over moderate heat until the fat runs, then continue cooking until the strips are crisp and brown. Stir occasionally during cooking.

Pour off the excess fat, then add the walnut oil, vinegar, mustard and seasoning to the bacon. Heat gently for 30 seconds, then spoon the bacon and dressing over the salads. Toss the leaves with the bacon and dressing and serve at once.

Salade de Flageolets
FLAGEOLET BEAN SALAD

You can use canned beans for this, but the flavour is definitely superior if you cook the dried beans in stock and turn them in the dressing while warm.

SERVES 6

225 G (8 OZ) DRIED FLAGEOLET BEANS

1.7 LITRES (3 PINTS) STOCK

1 BOUQUET GARNI

250 ML (8 FL OZ) MAYONNAISE (SEE PAGE 125)

30 ML (2 TBSP) CHOPPED FRESH PARSLEY

1 ONION, SKINNED AND FINELY CHOPPED

A LITTLE MILK OR CREAM (OPTIONAL)

Soak the beans overnight in plenty of cold water in a large saucepan. Drain the beans, then tip them back into the pan. Add the stock and bouquet garni. Bring to the boil, cover and simmer gently for about 1¼–1½ hours or until the beans are just tender; do not cook them until they begin to break.

Drain the beans. While they are still warm, stir in the mayonnaise, parsley and onion. Leave to cool for at least 2 hours before serving. If the dressing is then a little too thick when the beans have cooled, stir in the milk or cream.

Gougères
CHEESE CHOUX PUFFS

Although the term 'gougère' is widely used outside France for rings of choux pastry with a savoury filling, the authentic gougère is a small cheese-flavoured bun of choux paste, usually eaten warm or cold. The gougères should be larger than profiteroles: about the size of an individual Yorkshire pudding.

MAKES ABOUT 12

75 G (3 OZ) PLAIN FLOUR

1.25 ML (¼ TSP) SALT

FRESHLY MILLED BLACK PEPPER

50 G (2 OZ) BUTTER, CUT INTO CUBES

2 EGGS, BEATEN

75 G (3 OZ) GRUYÈRE CHEESE, FINELY GRATED

Sift the flour, salt and pepper together. Put the butter in a medium saucepan. Add 150 ml (¼ pint) water and heat very gently until the butter melts. When the butter has melted bring the liquid rapidly to the boil. Tip in the flour all at once, stirring. Remove the pan from the heat and stir until the mixture forms a ball of paste that leaves the sides of the pan clean. Do not over stir the mixture.

Allow the paste to cool for a few minutes, then gradually beat in the eggs. Continue beating until the paste is smooth and very glossy. Beat in the cheese.

Place about 12 spoonfuls of the paste well part on greased baking sheets. Bake at 220°C (425°F) mark 7 for 15 minutes. Reduce the oven temperature to 180°C (350°F) mark 4 and continue to cook for about 10-15 minutes, or until well risen, crisp and golden. Cool the gougères on a wire rack. Traditionally they are eaten warm or cold as a snack.

ANCHOÏADE

ANCHOVY PASTE

This Provençal speciality may be used in a number of ways. The most usual is to serve it hot, spread on pieces of toast with drinks or as a light snack. Alternatively, it may be served with vegetable crudités.

SERVES 4 AS A STARTER, OR 8 WITH DRINKS

1 LARGE GARLIC CLOVE

TWO 50 G (2 OZ) CANS ANCHOVY FILLETS IN OLIVE OIL

10 ML (2 TSP) LEMON JUICE

FRESHLY MILLED BLACK PEPPER

4 SLICES OF FRENCH BREAD, ABOUT 1 CM (½ INCH) THICK

Pound the garlic in a mortar, then add the anchovies together with the oil from the can and pound them until they form a coarse paste. Alternatively, crush the garlic in a food processor, add the anchovies and process quickly: the paste should not be too smooth. Stir in the lemon juice and season to taste with pepper.

Toast the bread on one side only. Spread the anchovy paste on the untoasted side of the hot bread, pressing it in well. Lay the slices in a small gratin dish. Cook at 230°C (450°F) mark 8 for about 4 minutes or heat the slices under a moderately hot grill. Serve immediately: the slices may be cut into small pieces to serve with drinks.

TAPÉNADE

OLIVES, ANCHOVY AND CAPER PASTE

A Provençal speciality, the name for this paste is derived from the local dialect – tapeno, *being the word for caper.*

SERVES 6

225 G (8 OZ) BLACK OLIVES, STONED

4 LARGE CANNED ANCHOVY FILLETS

GENEROUS 30 ML (2 TBSP) CAPERS

A LITTLE LEMON JUICE

60 ML (4 TBSP) VIRGIN OLIVE OIL

FRESHLY MILLED BLACK PEPPER

Purée the olives, anchovy fillets, capers and lemon juice in a blender or food processor until smooth. With the machine running, gradually pour in the olive oil in a thin, steady stream, as if making mayonnaise. Season to taste with pepper.

Pâtés and Terrines

Pâté de Campagne

COUNTRY-STYLE PÂTÉ

This pâté will keep well for up to a week in the refrigerator, so it is worth making a large quantity. It also freezes well.

SERVES 10–12

2 BAY LEAVES

12 RASHERS STREAKY BACON, RINDED

175G (6 OZ) FRESH WHITE BREADCRUMBS

2 EGGS

150 ML (¼ PINT) RED WINE

2 GARLIC CLOVES, CRUSHED

225 G (8 OZ) BELLY PORK, CUT INTO CHUNKS

225 G (8 OZ) FAT STREAKY OR FLANK BACON, RINDED

225 G (8 OZ) PORK LIVER, TRIMMED AND CUT INTO CHUNKS

450 G (1 LB) CHICKEN LIVERS, TRIMMED

10 ML (2 TSP) CHOPPED FRESH THYME

10 ML(2 TSP) CHOPPED FRESH SAGE

15 ML (1 TBSP) CHOPPED FRESH MARJORAM

30 ML (2 TBSP) CHOPPED FRESH PARSLEY

2.5 ML (½ TSP) GRATED NUTMEG

SALT AND FRESHLY MILLED BLACK PEPPER

Lightly grease a 1.5 litre (2½ pint) terrine and arrange the bay leaves on the base. Lay the bacon rashers one by one on a board and stretch them out thinly with the back of a knife. Line the base and sides of the terrine with the rashers.

Mix the breadcrumbs, eggs, wine and garlic. Finely mince the belly pork, streaky or flank bacon, pork and chicken livers. Alternatively, use a food processor to do this. Mix the minced meats and liver with the bread mixture. Add the herbs, nutmeg and plenty of seasoning. Turn the pâté mixture into the prepared terrine and fold over any ends of bacon rashers. Cover the pâté with foil and put the lid on the terrine.

Pour hot water into a large rectangular oven dish to a depth of 2.5 cm (1 inch). Stand the terrine in the dish and bake at 160°C (325°F) mark 3 for 2 hours.

Remove from the oven and place weights as evenly as possible on top of the foil. Allow the pâté to cool, then chill it overnight or for several hours. Remove the weights and turn the pâté out of the dish when ready to serve.

Terrine de Lièvre ou de Lapin

HARE OR RABBIT TERRINE

This terrine should be matured in the refrigerator for a couple of days before eating so that the flavours develop. Boning the hare or the rabbit is a rather long and tedious process but it is a great deal easier if you use a small, very sharp knife. The bones should be used to make stock.

SERVES 10–12

- 1 SMALL HARE OR LARGE RABBIT (ABOUT 2–2.7 KG [5–6 LB])
- 225 G (8 OZ) LEAN PORK, CUT INTO CHUNKS
- 225 G (8 OZ) FAT SALT PORK (IF SALT PORK IS NOT AVAILABLE SUBSTITUTE BACON), CUT INTO CHUNKS
- 1 LARGE ONION, SKINNED AND QUARTERED
- 30 ML (2 TBSP) CHOPPED FRESH PARSLEY
- 10 ML (2 TSP) CHOPPED FRESH THYME
- 6 JUNIPER BERRIES, CRUSHED
- 2 GARLIC CLOVES, CRUSHED
- SALT AND FRESHLY MILLED BLACK PEPPER
- 60 ML (4 TBSP) RED WINE
- 30 ML (2 TBSP) BRANDY
- 4 RASHERS SMOKED STREAKY BACON, RINDED

Bone the hare or rabbit and cut the meat from the back carefully into strips. Put the meat from the back carefully on one side. Mince the remainder with the fresh pork, salt pork or bacon and the onion. Alternatively use a food processor. Combine the minced ingredients with the parsley, thyme, juniper, garlic, seasoning, wine and brandy, and mix well.

Thoroughly grease a 1.5 litre (2½ pint) terrine. Place half the minced mixture in the base of the terrine, pressing it down evenly. Lay the reserved strips of meat and the rashers of streaky bacon on top, then spoon the remaining minced mixture into the terrine and smooth it down evenly.

Cover the pâté with a piece of greased foil and put the lid on the terrine. Pour hot water into a large rectangular oven dish to a depth of 2.5 cm (1 inch). Stand the terrine in the oven dish and bake at 160°C (325°F) mark 3 for 2½ hours.

Remove from the oven and place weights evenly on top of the foil. Allow to cool, then chill overnight or for several hours. Remove the weights and put the lid back on the terrine. Store in the refrigerator until required.

Overleaf: Left PÂTÉ DE CAMPAGNE *(see page 36), Centre* TERRINE DE LIÈVRE OU DE LAPIN *(above), Right* TERRINE DE POULET AU CITRON *(see page 40)*

Terrine de Poulet au Citron

CHICKEN TERRINE WITH LEMON AND WATERCRESS

A good, light terrine to serve as part of a buffet or for a summer lunch.

SERVES 8

1.4–1.8 KG (3–4 LB) CHICKEN WITH GIBLETS

225 G (8 OZ) BELLY PORK, CUT INTO CHUNKS

2 ONIONS, SKINNED AND QUARTERED

2 GARLIC CLOVES, CRUSHED

30 ML (2 TBSP) CHOPPED FRESH PARSLEY

10 ML (2 TSP) CHOPPED FRESH TARRAGON

GRATED RIND AND JUICE OF 1 SMALL LEMON

1 EGG, BEATEN

SALT AND FRESHLY MILLED BLACK PEPPER

BUNCH OF WATERCRESS

Reserve the liver and heart from the chicken giblets. Using a sharp, pointed knife, remove the breast meat from the chicken and cut it into neat strips; set aside. Remove all the remaining meat from the chicken carcass. The bones and skin are not required for this recipe but they may be used to make good stock for another purpose. Mince the chicken meat with the chicken liver and heart, pork and onions. Alternatively use a food processor. Put the minced mixture in a bowl and mix in the garlic, herbs, lemon rind and juice, and the egg. Add seasoning and mix well.

Thoroughly grease a 1.1 litre (2 pint) terrine. Pack half the mixture into it and lay the reserved strips of chicken breast on top. Season the strips. Cut off 2.5 cm (1 inch) of the watercress stalks, and chop the remainder finely. Scatter the chopped watercress over the chicken strips, then cover with the remaining minced mixture, packing it down neatly.

Place a piece of foil over the mixture and put the lid on the terrine. Pour hot water into a large rectangular oven dish to a depth of 2.5 cm (1 inch). Stand the terrine in the dish and cook at 160°C (325°F) mark 3 for 2 hours. Remove from the oven, drain off the liquid and place weights on top of the foil to press the chicken mixture while it cools. Remove the weights and serve the chicken terrine cut into slices.

TERRINE DE LÉGUMES

VEGETABLE TERRINE

This terrine is best served with Sauce de tomates *(see page 123), or a slightly piquant mayonnaise. Do make sure you season the spinach base really well as, during cooking, some of the other vegetables tend to absorb its seasoning.*

SERVES 8

40 G (1½ OZ) BUTTER

1 ONION, SKINNED AND CHOPPED

900 G (2 LB) SPINACH, STALKS REMOVED, WASHED

SALT AND FRESHLY MILLED BLACK PEPPER

75 G (3 OZ) FRESH WHITE OR BROWN BREADCRUMBS

3 EGGS, BEATEN

150 ML (¼ PINT) SINGLE CREAM OR CRÈME FRAÎCHE

3.75 ML (¾ TSP) GRATED NUTMEG

100 G (4 OZ) CAULIFLOWER FLORETS, BROKEN INTO SMALL PIECES

1 RED PEPPER, SEEDED AND CUT INTO STRIPS

100 G (4 OZ) CARROTS, PEELED AND CUT INTO 0.5 × 7.5 CM (¼ × 3 INCH) STRIPS

100 G (4OZ) BUTTON MUSHROOMS, SLICED

CAYENNE PEPPER

GOOD PINCH OF CARAWAY SEEDS

Melt the butter in a large saucepan. Add the onion and cook gently for 5 minutes. Drain the spinach, add to the pan and season with salt. Cover and cook gently for about 8 minutes, stirring once or twice, until the spinach is just tender. Drain the spinach well, pressing out all the water, then purée it in a blender or food processor. Mix the spinach purée with the breadcrumbs, eggs and cream. Add the nutmeg and seasoning.

Half fill a large saucepan with water, add 5 ml (1 tsp) salt and bring to the boil. Blanch the cauliflower, pepper and carrots in the boiling water by placing them in a sieve and plunging them into the saucepan for 1 minute. Remove from the pan, drain and add the next batch. Season the mushrooms with cayenne pepper. Sprinkle the caraway seeds over the blanched carrots and toss them lightly.

Line a 1.5 litre (2½ pint) terrine with non-stick baking parchment. Spread one fifth of the spinach mixture in the base of the terrine dish, then lay the strips of pepper on top. Cover with a quarter of the remaining spinach. Next, add a layer of mushrooms and top with a third of the remaining spinach. Arrange the carrots on top and cover with half of the remaining spinach. Lastly arrange the cauliflower in an even layer and top with the last of the spinach. Cover the mixture with a piece of non-stick baking parchment and put the lid on the terrine.

Pour hot water into a large rectangular oven dish to a depth of 2.5 cm (1 inch). Stand the terrine in the dish and cook at 180°C (350°F) mark 4 for 1 hour. Remove from the oven. Allow the terrine to cool, then chill it overnight. Remove from the refrigerator and turn out the vegetable terrine 15 minutes before serving.

Terrine de Poisson

FISH TERRINE

This makes a very elegant starter for a dinner party or it may be served as part of a selection of buffet dishes.

SERVES 10–12

WHITE FISH FARCE

1 BUNCH OF WATERCRESS

675 G (1½ LB) WHITE FISH FILLET (FOR EXAMPLE, WHITING, SOLE, TURBOT OR HALIBUT), SKINNED

7.5 ML (1½ TSP) SALT

ABOUT 1.25 ML (¼ TSP) GROUND WHITE PEPPER

1.25 ML (¼ TSP) GRATED NUTMEG

10 ML (2 TSP) CHOPPED FRESH TARRAGON

22.5 ML (1½ TBSP) LEMON JUICE

3 EGG WHITES

300 ML (½ PINT) SINGLE CREAM OR CRÈME FRAÎCHE

SALMON FARCE

350 G (12 OZ) SALMON FILLET, SKINNED

2.5 ML (½ TSP) SALT

FRESHLY MILLED BLACK PEPPER

GOOD PINCH OF GRATED NUTMEG

5 ML (1 TSP) ANCHOVY ESSENCE OR PURÉE

5 ML (1 TSP) TOMATO PURÉE

15 ML (1 TBSP) LEMON JUICE

1 EGG WHITE

150 ML (¼ PINT) SINGLE CREAM OR CRÈME FRAÎCHE

Cut off 2.5 cm (1 inch) of the watercress stalk. Finely chop the remainder. Purée the white fish in a blender or food processor with the salt, white pepper, nutmeg, tarragon and lemon juice until smooth. With the motor running, add the egg whites one at a time, then add the cream and process briefly until combined. Divide the mixture in half and stir the watercress into one portion.

Prepare the salmon farce as for the white fish farce, processing it first with the herbs and seasoning, then adding the egg white and finally the cream.

Line a 1.1 litre (2 pint) terrine with non-stick baking parchment. Put the watercress mixture into the base of the terrine and spread it out evenly. Carefully spoon the salmon farce on top, spreading it evenly and taking care not to mix the two layers. Finally spoon the white fish farce on top and spread it evenly. Cover the mixture with a piece of non-stick baking parchment and put the lid on the terrine.

Pour hot water into a large rectangular oven dish to a depth of 2.5 cm (1 inch). Stand the terrine in the dish and cook at 160°C (325°F) mark 3 for 1 hour or until the fish mixture is firm. Remove from the oven.

Allow the terrine to cool, then chill it in the refrigerator overnight. Invert the terrine on to a serving dish and cut it into slices to serve.

TERRINE DE POISSON

Terrine de Porc et de Veau

PORK AND VEAL TERRINE

SERVES 6–8

450 G (1 LB) LEAN PORK, MINCED

450 G (1 LB) LEAN VEAL, MINCED

225 G (8 OZ) SMOKED BACON IN ONE PIECE

5 ML (1 TSP) SALT

5 ML (1 TSP) CRUSHED BLACK PEPPERCORNS

6 JUNIPER BERRIES, CRUSHED

60 ML (4 TBSP) SHERRY

4 RASHERS SMOKED STREAKY BACON

3 BAY LEAVES

Mix together the pork and veal. Chop the smoked bacon piece with a little fat if available. Add this to the meats with the salt, peppercorns, juniper berries and sherry. Leave to stand for 1 hour in order for the flavours to mix.

Transfer to a greased 1.1 litre (2 pint) pâté terrine dish, pressing it down well (as it tends to shrink during cooking). Remove the rind from the bacon rashers and cut into thin strips. Arrange in a lattice pattern over the top of the terrine. Press the bay leaves into the bacon. Cover with the lid and cook at 160°C (325°F) mark 3 for 1 hour. Remove the lid and cook for a further 30 minutes. Remove from the oven and allow to cool thoroughly, then chill for several hours before serving thickly sliced.

Pâté de Foie de Volaille

CHICKEN, DUCK OR TURKEY LIVER PÂTÉ

One of the quickest and easiest pâtés to make, this recipe is also one that is always popular. For a lighter pâté, beat in 100 g (4 oz) of curd cheese after the liver has been mixed with the last of the butter.

SERVES 4

150 G (5 OZ) BUTTER

1 SMALL ONION, SKINNED AND VERY FINELY CHOPPED

1 GARLIC CLOVE, CRUSHED

1 THYME SPRIG

225 G (8 OZ) CHICKEN, DUCK OR TURKEY LIVERS, TRIMMED

15 ML (1 TBSP) BRANDY

SALT AND FRESHLY MILLED BLACK PEPPER

Melt 25 g (1 oz) of the butter in a small frying pan. Add the onion, garlic and thyme and cook gently for 5 minutes. Add the liver and cook it quickly, for about 5 minutes, stirring frequently. Remove the pan from the heat and allow the mixture to cool slightly. Discard the thyme. Purée all the cooked ingredients in a blender or a food processor until smooth. Soften 75 g (3 oz) of the remaining butter, then gradually beat in the liver purée. Stir in the brandy and seasoning to taste. Pack the pâté into a small pot or dish. Melt the remaining butter in a small saucepan, allow it to cool slightly, then strain it over the pâté. Leave the pâté to cool, then chill it lightly before serving with thin, crisp toast.

Fish and Shellfish

Paupiettes de Sole au Vermouth

PAUPIETTES OF SOLE WITH SCALLOPS AND VERMOUTH

To prepare scallops bought in the shell, first select those with tightly closed shells. Rest the hinge of the shell on a flat surface and insert a small knife into one of the openings on either side of the shell, just above the hinge. Prise open slightly and, keeping the knife close against the flat shell, sever the muscle attaching the meat to the shell. Remove the scallop meat and discard the black sac and remaining muscle.

SERVES 4

8 FILLETS OF LEMON SOLE, SKINNED

8 SCALLOPS

300 ML (½ PINT) VERMOUTH

FEW FRESH FENNEL LEAF SPRIGS

FEW FRESH PARSLEY STALKS

1 BAY LEAF

SALT AND FRESHLY MILLED BLACK PEPPER

SAUCE

25 G (1 OZ) BUTTER

1 SHALLOT, SKINNED AND FINELY CHOPPED

25 G (1 OZ) PLAIN FLOUR

5 ML (1 TSP) CHOPPED FRESH FENNEL

5 ML (1 TSP) CHOPPED FRESH PARSLEY

30 ML (2 TBSP) CREAM

Roll each sole fillet around a scallop and secure with a wooden cocktail stick. Place the paupiettes into a marmitout skillet (see page 65) or small frying pan, add the vermouth, herbs and seasoning. Cover with a piece of buttered paper or foil and poach gently for 10–12 minutes or until the fish is tender. Carefully strain off the cooking liquor into a jug and keep the fish hot. Discard the herbs.

Melt the butter in the marmitout pan or a saucepan. Add the shallot and gently fry until very soft but not coloured. Add the flour and cook until all the butter is absorbed. Remove the pan from the heat. Make up the fish liquor to 450 ml (¾ pint) with sufficient water. Stir into the pan and cook until thickened. Add the herbs and seasoning to taste.

Finally, stir in the cream but do not allow the sauce to boil. Remove the sticks from the fish, return the marmitout or pan to the heat and gently reheat the fish in the sauce.

COQUILLES ST JACQUES À L'ESTRAGON

STEAMED SCALLOPS WITH CREAM AND TARRAGON SAUCE

In this recipe, the scallops are steamed in cling film (use the kind that is advised as suitable for microwave cookers) – a technique that is used extensively in the top restaurants in the world. It ensures that all the natural juices of the fish are preserved.

SERVES 4

25 G (1 OZ) BUTTER

1 SHALLOT, SKINNED AND FINELY CHOPPED

300 ML (½ PINT) WHITE WINE

300 ML (½ PINT) DOUBLE CREAM

10 ML (2 TSP) FINELY CHOPPED FRESH TARRAGON

SALT AND FRESHLY MILLED BLACK PEPPER

450 G (1 LB) PREPARED SCALLOPS

First make the sauce. Melt the butter in the small saucepan. Add the shallot and fry gently until soft. Add the wine and boil rapidly until reduced to about 45 ml (3 tbsp). Add the cream and tarragon. Bring to the boil and boil until reduced by about half. Remove from the heat, season and set aside. Take two pieces of cling film, about 50 cm (20 inches) long, and place half the scallops in the centre of each. Bring the short sides together and fold them over until they are tight, then twist the ends together to make a neat bag from which all the air has been excluded. Make a knot in each end.

Half fill the large saucepan with water and bring to the boil. Gently reheat the sauce. Carefully place the two scallop bags in the gently simmering water and poach for about 3 minutes or until just cooked; do not overcook them. Place the scallop bags in a heated bowl and make a slit in each bag. Pour all the juices into the sauce, bring to the boil and boil rapidly until the sauce is reduced to the consistency of double cream. Pour on to a heated serving dish and arrange the scallops on top.

GRATIN DE CREVETTES

GRATIN OF PRAWNS

SERVES 4

15 ML (1 TBSP) OLIVE OIL

4 SHALLOTS, SKINNED AND CHOPPED

2 GARLIC CLOVES, CRUSHED

2 MEDIUM CARROTS, PEELED AND CUT INTO SMALL DICE

4 TOMATOES, SKINNED AND CHOPPED

150 ML (¼ PINT) WHITE WINE

225 G (8 OZ) PEELED PRAWNS

SALT AND FRESHLY MILLED BLACK PEPPER

100 G (4 OZ) FIRM MUSHROOMS, SLICED

SAUCE

25 G (1 OZ) BUTTER

25 G (1 OZ) PLAIN FLOUR

300 ML (½ PINT) MILK

100 G (4 OZ) HARD CHEESE, GRATED

A LITTLE GRATED NUTMEG

Heat the oil in a frying pan. Add the shallots, garlic and carrots and gently fry until softened but not browned. Add the tomatoes and white wine and simmer gently for 10 minutes, or until all the vegetables are tender. Add the prawns, then raise the heat so that the liquid reduces by half. Season to taste. Divide between four buttered dishes and top with mushrooms.

To make the sauce, melt the butter in a small saucepan, add the flour and cook for 1–2 minutes without colouring. Remove from the heat and add the milk, a little at a time. Return to the heat and cook until thickened, stirring. Add two-thirds of the cheese, a little nutmeg and seasoning. Pour over the top of the vegetable and prawn mixture. Sprinkle the remaining cheese over the top. Cook at 200°C (400°F) mark 6 for 20–25 minutes.

Saumon aux Poireaux

SALMON WITH LEEK

In this dish the leeks are cooked separately and then served with the salmon, together with its creamy sauce.

SERVES 4

50 G (2 OZ) BUTTER

3 MEDIUM LEEKS, WHITE PARTS ONLY, FINELY SLICED

300 G (11 OZ) WHITE PART OF LEEKS, FINELY SLICED

SALT AND FRESHLY MILLED BLACK PEPPER

75 G (3 OZ) SHALLOTS, SKINNED AND CHOPPED

100 G (4 OZ) MUSHROOMS, SLICED

150 ML (¼ PINT) DRY WHITE WINE

4 SALMON STEAKS

300 ML (½ PINT) CRÈME FRAÎCHE

15–30 ML (1–2 TBSP) CHOPPED FRESH CHERVIL

Melt half the butter in a medium saucepan. Stir in the leeks, then pour in 75 ml (3 fl oz) water and add some seasoning. Simmer the leeks gently for 20 minutes.

Melt the remaining butter in a rectangular oven dish on the hob. Add the shallots and cook them gently for 5 minutes. Stir in the mushrooms and cook gently for 2 minutes. Pour in the wine and add seasoning. Turn the heat off and arrange the salmon steaks in the dish. Cover and bake the salmon steaks at 200°C (400°F) mark 6 for 7–10 minutes, until they are just cooked.

Transfer the steaks to four plates and keep hot. Put the baking dish on the hob and boil the cooking liquor rapidly until it is reduced by half. Add the crème fraîche and boil until the sauce is reduced and slightly thickened. Strain this sauce.

Arrange the leeks on the plates with the salmon steaks, then add some of the sauce. Garnish with chopped chervil and serve. Hand any remaining sauce separately.

Friture

DORDOGNE – STYLE FRIED FISH

Tiny fish abound in the rivers and streams of the Dordogne where the local fishermen often fry them over an open fire. The simply cooked fish is then sprinkled with chopped parsley, lemon rind and finely chopped onion, and eaten piping hot. Any small fish can be used for this dish, but whitebait are the most easily obtainable.

SERVES 4

60 ML (4 TBSP) CHOPPED FRESH PARSLEY

GRATED RIND OF 1 LARGE LEMON

1 MEDIUM ONION, SKINNED AND VERY FINELY CHOPPED

30 ML (2 TBSP) PLAIN FLOUR

SALT AND FRESHLY MILLED BLACK PEPPER

450 G (1 LB) WHITEBAIT

45 ML(3 TBSP) VEGETABLE OIL

25 G (1 OZ) BUTTER

TO SERVE: LEMON WEDGES

Mix the parsley, lemon rind and onion, then set aside. Mix the flour and seasoning in a bowl and toss the fish lightly in it.

Heat the oil and butter in a large non-stick frying pan. Add the whitebait and cook until it is golden brown all over, turning frequently. Scatter the parsley mixture over the fish and serve at once, garnished with lemon wedges for their juice.

Cabillaud aux Tomates

COD WITH TOMATOES

Cod may be considered a fairly humble fish, however, when it is perfectly fresh and well-cooked it rivals many of the more expensive varieties.

SERVES 4

50 G (2 OZ) BUTTER

SALT AND FRESHLY MILLED BLACK PEPPER

4 COD CUTLETS

1 ONION, SKINNED AND CHOPPED

1 GARLIC CLOVE, CRUSHED

450 G (1 LB) TOMATOES, SKINNED, QUARTERED AND SEEDED

75 ML (5 TBSP) DRY WHITE WINE

22.5 ML (1½ TBSP) CHOPPED FRESH BASIL

Melt the butter in a large frying pan. Season the fish and cook the cutlets gently in the butter for about 12 minutes, turning once. Transfer the cooked fish to a heated serving dish, cover and keep hot.

Add the onion and garlic to the butter remaining in the pan and cook gently for 10 minutes. Add the tomatoes to the pan and cook for a further 3 minutes, then stir in the wine and bring to the boil. Season, lower the heat and simmer gently for 5 minutes. Spoon the tomato mixture over the fish and sprinkle with the basil. Serve at once.

Rougets au Basilic

BAKED RED MULLET WITH BASIL

Basil loses its flavour very quickly once it has been chopped, so it is important to chop it and sprinkle it over the fish just as it is being served.

SERVES 4

4 RED MULLET, CLEANED

90 ML (6 TBSP) VIRGIN OLIVE OIL

60 ML (4 TBSP) LEMON JUICE

2 GARLIC CLOVES, CRUSHED

SALT AND FRËHLY MILLED BLACK PEPPER

8 SLICES OF LEMON

30 ML (2 TBSP) CHOPPED FRESH BASIL

Take four pieces of foil, each large enough to enclose a fish. Brush the foil with some of the oil and place the mullet in the centre. Mix the remaining oil, lemon juice, garlic and seasoning. Spoon this mixture over the fish and lay a couple of lemon slices on top of each fish.

Fold the sides of the foil up to enclose each fish in a neat package. Place these in a large oval gratin dish and bake at 180°C (350°F) mark 4 for 30 minutes. Open the foil packages and sprinkle the basil over the fish. Serve immediately, leaving each fish in its part-opened package.

Overleaf: Left ROUGETS AU BASILIC *(above), Centre* SAUMON AUX POIREAUX *(see page 48), Right* LOTTE DE MER AU FENOUIL *(see page 57)*

Truites aux Chanterelles en Papillotes

TROUT AND MUSHROOM PARCELS

Cooking in paper parcels is a well-established method of keeping food moist and it is ideal for whole fish such as trout, perch or mackerel.

SERVES 4

4 TROUT, CLEANED

SALT AND FRESHLY MILLED BLACK PEPPER

50 G (2 OZ) BUTTER PLUS EXTRA FOR GREASING

2 SHALLOTS, SKINNED AND FINELY CHOPPED

225 G (8 OZ) CHANTERELLES OR BUTTON MUSHROOMS, FINELY CHOPPED

30 ML (2 TBSP) CHOPPED FRESH DILL, OR PARSLEY

60 ML (4 TBSP) DRY WHITE WINE

Cut four pieces of greaseproof paper, each large enough to enclose a fish. Sprinkle the trout inside and out with seasoning. Butter the pieces of paper, then lay a fish on each sheet. Melt the butter in a small saucepan. Add the shallots, chanterelles and dill, and cook gently for about 8 minutes.

Divide the mushroom mixture between the fish. Carefully pour 15 ml (1 tbsp) wine over one fish, fold up the paper to enclose it. Fold the edges two or three times, so that the fish is completely enclosed and the juices cannot escape. Place the package in a large rectangular oven dish. Add wine to the remaining fish, pack them and put them in the dish.

Bake at 225°C (425°F) mark 7 for 15 minutes. Serve the parcels in the dish, opening the paper a little so that the contents are visible.

Raie au Beurre Noir

SKATE WITH BLACK BUTTER

The ribbed flesh of skate has a pleasant flavour in this simple classic dish that is quick to prepare.

SERVES 4

4 PIECES OF SKATE WING

SALT AND FRESHLY MILLED BLACK PEPPER

300 ML (½ PINT) DRY WHITE WINE

2 SHALLOTS, SKINNED AND CHOPPED

FEW PARSLEY OR CHERVIL SPRIGS

100 G (4 OZ) BUTTER

15 ML (1 TBSP) WHITE WINE VINEGAR

Cook the seasoned skate wings, two at a time in a large frying pan, with the wine, shallots and herbs. Baste them with the wine during cooking. Cook for about 10 minutes, or until tender. Remove the skate to a serving dish and keep hot. Pour off the cooking liquor and retain as fish stock for another recipe.

Wipe out the pan. Add the butter, heat until lightly browned, then add the vinegar. Pour immediately over the skate wings.

Marmite de Sole et de Moules

CASSEROLE OF SOLE AND MUSSELS

Sole and mussels make an excellent combination in this quickly prepared seafood casserole.

SERVES 4

25 G (1 OZ) BUTTER

30 ML (2 TBSP) OLIVE OIL

1 MEDIUM ONION, SKINNED AND CHOPPED

1 LEEK, TRIMMED AND SLICED

1 SMALL BULB FENNEL, SLICED

1 CELERY STICK, SLICED

1 GARLIC CLOVE, CRUSHED

15 ML (1 TBSP) CHOPPED FRESH THYME

2 LARGE TOMATOES, SKINNED AND SLICED

300 ML (½ PINT) DRY WHITE WINE

300 ML (½ PINT) FISH STOCK

900 G (2 LB) MUSSELS

4 FILLETS OF SOLE

SALT AND FRESHLY MILLED BLACK PEPPER

A PINCH OF CAYENNE

2.5 ML (½ TSP) POWDERED SAFFRON

60 ML (4 TBSP) DOUBLE CREAM

Heat the butter and oil in a buffet casserole or large shallow casserole. Add the onion, leek, fennel and celery and gently fry until softened but not browned. Add the garlic, thyme, tomatoes, wine and fish stock. Wash and scrub the mussels well, discarding any that are open, and remove the beards (see page 57). Add the mussels to the casserole, cover and simmer for 15–20 minutes or until all the shells are open. Lift out the mussels and remove them from their shells. Continue cooking the vegetables until soft. Press the vegetables and liquid through a sieve back into the casserole. Boil to reduce by one third. Cut the sole crossways into slices about 2.5 cm (1 inch) thick. Add to the sauce and simmer for about 10 minutes. Add seasoning, cayenne and saffron. Add the cream and return the mussels to reheat.

Sole au Papaye

SOLE WITH PAWPAW

SERVES 4

8 FILLETS LEMON SOLE, SKINNED

FINELY GRATED RIND OF 1 LEMON

8 SPRIGS OF FRESH DILL, OR 5 ML (1 TSP) DRIED DILL

SALT

FRESHLY MILLED BLACK PEPPER

25 G (1 OZ) BUTTER

150 ML (¼ PINT) DRY WHITE WINE

JUICE OF 1 LEMON

1 MEDIUM PAWPAW

30 ML (2 TBSP) DOUBLE CREAM

5 ML (1 TSP) SUGAR IF REQUIRED

Lay the fillets on a board and sprinkle each with a little of the lemon rind. Add the sprigs of dill or sprinkle each one with a little of the dried dill. Season and roll up. Melt the butter in a gratin dish, and add the wine, lemon juice and a little seasoning. Peel the pawpaw, cut in half lengthways and remove the seeds. Cut the fruit into thin slices and add to the liquid. Stand the rolls of fish in the liquid and cover with greased greaseproof paper or foil. Poach gently for 10–12 minutes or until the fish is tender. Remove the fish and keep hot on a warmed serving dish. Transfer all the cooking liquid to an electric blender and liquidize until smooth. Return the sauce to the gratin dish, add the cream and check the seasoning, adding the sugar if required. Heat gently, without boiling, before serving around the fish.

Daurade à la Sauce de Poivron Rouge

SEA BREAM WITH RED PEPPER SAUCE

The red pepper sauce which accompanies the fish in this dish has a delicate, mellow flavour.

SERVES 4

4 MEDIUM SEA BREAM, CLEANED

MARINADE DE CITRON (SEE PAGE 130)

1 LARGE RED PEPPER

45 ML (3 TBSP) OLIVE OIL

SALT AND FRESHLY MILLED BLACK PEPPER

TO GARNISH: LEMON WEDGES

Lay the bream in a large oval gratin dish. Pour the marinade over the fish, cover and leave to marinate for 2–3 hours.

Meanwhile, place the pepper in a small round gratin dish and put it under a hot grill. Cook the pepper, turning it occasionally, until the skin is charred. Set aside until cool enough to handle. Peel off all the skin of the pepper and discard the seeds. Purée the pepper flesh in a blender or food processor until smooth. Leave the purée in the machine.

Lift the fish out of the marinade. Strain the liquor and gradually add it to the pepper purée with the machine running. When the marinade is incorporated, slowly trickle in the oil in the same way. Season the mixture to taste, then pour it into a small saucepan and heat it gently. Heat a grill and cook the fish for about 8–10 minutes, turning once. Transfer the fish to a heated serving dish. Add any grilling juices from the fish to the sauce, stir them in, and pour the sauce over the fish. Garnish with lemon wedges and serve at once.

Saumon au Beurre de Fenouil

SALMON STEAKS WITH FENNEL BUTTER

Simple grilled salmon, topped with fennel butter, with the flavour of the dish improved by a dash of Pernod.

SERVES 4

50 G (2 OZ) BUTTER

30 ML (2 TBSP) CHOPPED FRESH FENNEL LEAVES

A GOOD SQUEEZE OF LEMON JUICE

SALT AND FRESHLY MILLED BLACK PEPPER

4 SALMON STEAKS

15 ML (1 TBSP) VEGETABLE OIL

15 ML (1 TBSP) PERNOD

TO GARNISH: FENNEL SPRIGS

Cream the butter and beat in the fennel, lemon juice and pepper to taste. Place the butter on a piece of cling film or damp greaseproof paper, shape it into a roll, then wrap it neatly and chill well. Season the salmon steaks on both sides.

Brush a grill with the oil and put it over moderate heat. When the grill is hot place the salmon steaks on it and cook them for 5 minutes. Turn the steaks and cook them for a further 5 minutes. Pour the Pernod over the steaks and set it alight. As soon as the flames have died down, lift the steaks off the grill and arrange them on a serving dish. Pour over all the cooking juices from the pan and top each steak with a pat of butter. Garnish with sprigs of fennel and serve at once.

DAURADE À LA SAUCE DE POIVRON ROUGE

Merlans aux Légumes

WHITING WITH VEGETABLES

Other fish such as haddock, plaice or monkfish may be used in place of whiting in this dish.

SERVES 4

40 G (1½ OZ) BUTTER

2 LEEKS, TRIMMED AND THINLY SLICED

2 CELERY STICKS, THINLY SLICED

3 CARROTS, PEELED AND CUT INTO MATCHSTICK STRIPS

100 G (4 OZ) BUTTON MUSHROOMS

4 WHITING, FILLETED, OR 8 WHITING FILLETS

SALT AND FRESHLY MILLED BLACK PEPPER

150 ML (¼ PINT) DRY WHITE WINE

15 G (½ OZ) PLAIN FLOUR

150 ML (¼ PINT) SINGLE CREAM

Melt 25 g (1 oz) of the butter in a large gratin dish, add the leeks, celery and carrots and cook gently until they are all beginning to soften. Add the mushrooms and continue cooking for about 5 minutes over a low heat. Lift out the vegetables. Remove the gratin dish from the heat. Lay the fish fillets in the dish and season. Scatter the vegetables over the top. Pour the wine and 150 ml (¼ pint) water over the fish and cover tightly with foil. Bake at 160°C (325°F) mark 3 for 40 minutes. Meanwhile, beat the remaining butter and flour together to make a smooth paste or *beurre manié*. Use a fish slice to carefully lift the fish and vegetables from the dish and place it on a heated serving dish. Cover and keep hot. Bring the cooking liquor to the boil on the hob.

Whisk the liquid all the time as you add the *beurre manié* a teaspoonful at a time. When all the paste is added and melted into the liquid, simmer the sauce for about 2 minutes, until thickened. Reduce the heat and stir in the cream. Heat gently without allowing the sauce to boil. Taste and adjust the seasoning, then spoon the sauce over the fish and vegetables, and serve at once.

Sardines aux Épinards

SARDINES WITH SPINACH

An inexpensive supper dish which will prove extremely popular.

SERVES 3–4

900 G (2 LB) SPINACH, WASHED

SALT AND FRESHLY MILLED BLACK PEPPER

60 ML (4 TBSP) OLIVE OIL

1 LARGE ONION, SKINNED AND FINELY CHOPPED

2 GARLIC CLOVES, CRUSHED

450 G (1 LB) FRESH SARDINES, CLEANED WITH HEADS REMOVED

30 ML (2 TBSP) FRESH WHITE BREADCRUMBS

Place the spinach in a large saucepan. Add 45 ml (3 tbsp) water and a little salt. Bring to the boil, then cook the spinach for 10 minutes or until it is tender. Drain the spinach thoroughly, squeezing out the water, and chop it finely.

Heat 30 ml (2 tbsp) of the oil in a medium saucepan. Add the onion and garlic, and cook gently for about 5 minutes. Stir in the spinach and seasoning until well mixed. Turn the mixture into a medium gratin dish.

Season the sardines and lay them on top of the spinach. Sprinkle the breadcrumbs over the top, then trickle the remaining oil over the crumbs. Bake at 190°C (375°F) mark 5 for 15–20 minutes.

MOULES AU GRATIN

MUSSELS WITH GARLIC AND BREADCRUMBS

Be careful not to overcook the mussels for this dish, either when cooking initially or when grilling, or they can become dry and slightly tough.

SERVES 4–6 AS A MAIN COURSE, 8 AS AN HORS D'OEUVRE

2 KG (4¼ LB) MUSSELS

1 ONION, SKINNED AND CHOPPED

A FEW PARSLEY STALKS

1 THYME SPRIG

100 G (4 OZ) BUTTER

10 ML (2 TSP) LEMON JUICE

2 GARLIC CLOVES, CRUSHED

45 ML (3 TBSP) CHOPPED FRESH PARSLEY

50 G (2 OZ) FRESH WHITE BREADCRUMBS

40 G (1½ OZ) FRESHLY GRATED PARMESAN CHEESE

Put the mussels to soak in fresh cold water for about 2 hours; ridding the shellfish of sand and excess salt. Scrub the mussels, remove all the traces of seaweed and mud. Pull away the black, hairy beard. Discard any which are cracked or shells that are open and do not close when sharply tapped.

Put the onion, parsley stalks and thyme into a large cocotte. Pour in 300 ml (½ pint) water and bring to the boil. Simmer, covered, for 5 minutes. Add the mussels, cover and cook quickly, shaking the pan constantly. As soon as the mussels open, remove from the heat and leave until cool enough to handle.

Discard the empty half of each shell and place the mussels in their shells in a single layer in two large oval gratin dishes. Melt the butter in a small saucepan over a gentle heat.

Remove from the heat, then stir in the lemon juice and garlic. Spoon this over the mussels and scatter the parsley on top. Mix the breadcrumbs and Parmesan, then sprinkle the mixture over the mussels. Grill for about 3 minutes or until the breadcrumbs are golden.

LOTTE DE MER AU FENOUIL

MONKFISH IN FENNEL

The firm flesh of monkfish has no bones, once the thick backbone has been removed.

SERVES 4

30 ML (2 TBSP) OLIVE OIL

1 FENNEL BULB, THINLY SLICED

2 CELERY STICKS, THINLY SLICED

6 SHALLOTS, SKINNED AND CHOPPED

900 G (2 LB) MONKFISH, CUT INTO THICK SLICES

SALT AND FRESHLY MILLED BLACK PEPPER

300 ML (½ PINT) PERNOD

100 G (4 OZ) BUTTER, CUT INTO SMALL PIECES

15 ML (1 TBSP) CHOPPED FRESH BASIL

10 ML (2 TSP) CORNFLOUR

Heat the oil in a large gratin dish. Add the fennel, celery and shallots and gently fry the vegetables until softened but not browned. Lift them out, draining well. Brown the pieces of fish in the oil, then remove. Replace the vegetables and lay the fish on top, season and add 150 ml (¼ pint) of the Pernod. Cover and cook at 200°C (400°F) mark 6 for 30–40 minutes, or until the fish and vegetables are tender.

Meanwhile, put the remaining Pernod in a small saucepan and add the butter, stirring all the time. When the fish is cooked, carefully strain off the cooking liquor and add this to the sauce together with the basil. Blend the cornflour with a little water and stir into the sauce. Bring to the boil, then adjust the seasoning. Pour the sauce over the fish just before serving.

Moules au Cidre

MUSSELS IN CIDER

Excellent mussels are gathered off the coast of Brittany where they are cooked as frequently in cider as in wine. For this recipe it really is essential that the mussels are soaked for a couple of hours before using or the sauce will be too salty.

SERVES 4–6

4 SHALLOTS, SKINNED AND CHOPPED

A FEW PARSLEY STALKS

1 THYME SPRIG

1 BAY LEAF

A FEW BLACK PEPPERCORNS

300 ML (½ PINT) DRY CIDER

2 KG (4¼ LB) MUSSELS, CLEANED (SEE PAGE 57)

150 ML (¼ PINT) DOUBLE CREAM

15 ML (1 TBSP) CHOPPED FRESH CHIVES

Put the shallots into a buffet casserole with the parsley stalks, thyme, bay leaf, peppercorns and cider. Bring slowly to the boil, cover and simmer gently for 5 minutes. Add the mussels, cover and cook quickly, shaking the pan constantly, until all the mussels have opened. Strain all the cooking liquor into a medium saucepan. Cover the casserole and keep the mussels warm.

Boil the cooking liquor rapidly until it is reduced to just under 300 ml (½ pint). Stir in the cream and heat together. Taste and adjust the seasoning. Pour the sauce over the mussels, sprinkle with the chives and serve at once.

Thon à la Sauce Tomate

TUNA WITH TOMATO SAUCE

Although fresh tuna is now more readily available, you may have to order it from your fishmonger.

SERVES 4

30 ML (2 TBSP) OLIVE OIL

4 MEDIUM FRESH TUNA STEAKS

4 SHALLOTS, SKINNED AND CHOPPED

2 GARLIC CLOVES, CRUSHED

4 LARGE TOMATOES, SKINNED AND CHOPPED

1 BOUQUET GARNI

150 ML (¼ PINT) RED WINE

150 ML (¼ PINT) FISH STOCK OR WATER

1 ANCHOVY, CHOPPED

SALT AND FRESHLY MILLED BLACK PEPPER

15 G (½ OZ) BUTTER

10 ML (2 TSP) PLAIN FLOUR

15 ML (1 TBSP) CHOPPED FRESH PARSLEY

Heat the oil in a large gratin dish. Add the tuna and fry on both sides until golden. Remove from the dish. Add the shallots and garlic and gently fry until soft. Carefully drain off the excess oil. Add the tomatoes, bouquet garni, wine, stock and anchovy to the dish. Place the tuna on top of the vegetables and season well.

Cover and cook for 30 minutes. Remove the bouquet garni and tuna, keeping the tuna hot. Blend the butter and flour together until smooth to make a beurre manié. Put the gratin dish over a medium heat and stir in small pieces of the beurre manié. Cook until the sauce thickens, stirring. Replace the tuna and sprinkle with the parsley.

MOULES AU CIDRE

Langoustine au Beurre d'Ail

GRILLED PRAWNS WITH GARLIC BUTTER

The prawns are grilled in their shells to keep them moist.

SERVES 4 AS A STARTER

12–16 UNCOOKED KING PRAWNS

JUICE OF 1 LEMON

45 ML (3 TBSP) OLIVE OIL

2 GARLIC CLOVES, CRUSHED

FRESHLY MILLED BLACK PEPPER

50 G (2 OZ) BUTTER

30 ML (2 TBSP) CHOPPED FRESH PARSLEY

Remove the heads from the prawns, if necessary. Lay the prawns in a gratin dish. Mix half the lemon juice, the olive oil, one clove of garlic and the pepper, then pour this mixture over the prawns. Cover and leave to marinate for 1–2 hours.

Heat a meat grill. Lift the prawns out of the marinade and cook them on the grill for about 6 minutes, turning once. While the prawns are cooking, put the remaining garlic, lemon juice, butter and parsley into a small saucepan and heat gently, stirring occasionally.

Transfer the prawns to a heated serving dish and pour the butter mixture over them. Serve at once.

Soufflé au Crabe

CRAB SOUFFLÉ

If the soufflé is baked in a fan-assisted oven, it will be cooked after about 45 minutes.

SERVES 4

40 G (1½ OZ) BUTTER PLUS EXTRA FOR GREASING

40 G (1½ OZ) PLAIN FLOUR

300 ML (½ PINT) MILK

6 EGGS, SIZE 1, SEPARATED

60 ML (4 TBSP) CANNED LOBSTER BISQUE

SALT AND FRESHLY MILLED BLACK PEPPER

200 G (7 OZ) CAN WHITE CRAB MEAT, DRAINED

Melt the butter in a large saucepan. Stir in the flour, then cook gently for 2 minutes, stirring all the time. Gradually pour in the milk, stirring vigorously, and bring the sauce to the boil. Stir continuously to prevent the sauce from sticking: it should be thick and quite smooth.

Take the saucepan off the heat, then beat in the egg yolks one at a time. Stir in the lobster bisque and seasoning, then mix in the crab meat.

Thoroughly butter a 2.5 litre (4¼ pint) soufflé dish. Whisk the egg whites until they stand in firm peaks but do not overwhisk them until they are dry. Add a small spoonful of the whites to the crab mixture and beat it in to soften the sauce. Carefully fold in the remaining whites. Turn the mixture into the dish. Bake at 160°C (325°F) mark 3 for 1 hour, until risen and golden. Serve at once.

Calmars aux Tomates et au Cognac

SQUID WITH TOMATOES AND COGNAC

Buy fresh or frozen ready-prepared squid if possible.

SERVES 4

- 30 ML (2 TBSP) OLIVE OIL
- 1 MEDIUM ONION, SKINNED AND CHOPPED
- 2 GARLIC CLOVES, CRUSHED
- 900 G (2 LB) SMALL SQUID, CUT INTO BITE-SIZE PIECES
- 30 ML (2 TBSP) COGNAC
- 450 G (1 LB) TOMATOES, SKINNED AND CHOPPED
- 300 ML (½ PINT) DRY WHITE WINE
- BOUQUET GARNI
- SALT AND FRESHLY MILLED BLACK PEPPER
- FEW STRIPS OF ORANGE RIND
- 15 ML (1 TBSP) CHOPPED FRESH PARSLEY

Heat the olive oil in a buffet casserole or large gratin dish. Add the onion and garlic and gently fry until softened but not browned. Add the squid and cook until all the liquid has evaporated, stirring occasionally. Add the cognac and flambé for a few moments.

Stir in the tomatoes, wine, bouquet garni, seasoning and orange rind. Cover and cook gently for about 1 hour or until the pieces of squid are tender. Remove the bouquet garni and orange rind before serving. Sprinkle with the parsley.

Oeufs Brouilles aux Langoustines

SCRAMBLED EGGS WITH PRAWNS

This quick and easy dish is perfect for lunch or supper.

SERVES 2

- 50 G (2 OZ) BUTTER
- 6 LARGE PRAWNS
- 3 EGGS
- SALT AND FRESHLY MILLED BLACK PEPPER
- 2.5 ML (½ TSP) PAPRIKA
- 30 ML (2 TBSP) DOUBLE CREAM

Divide the butter and heat in two egg dishes. Lightly fry half the prawns in each dish. Lift out and keep hot. Beat the eggs with the seasoning, paprika and double cream and lightly scramble in the two dishes. When cooked, mix in the prawns and serve immediately.

Poultry and Game

Poulet aux Olives

CHICKEN WITH OLIVES AND TOMATOES

The saffron in this dish not only gives colour, but a distinctive flavour to it.

SERVES 6

6 CHICKEN QUARTERS OR 12 CHICKEN THIGHS

SALT AND FRESHLY MILLED BLACK PEPPER

30 ML (2 TBSP) PLAIN FLOUR

45 ML (3 TBSP) OLIVE OIL

225 G (8 OZ) BUTTON ONIONS, SKINNED

2 GARLIC CLOVES, CRUSHED

450 G (1 LB) TOMATOES, SKINNED

100–175 G (4–6 OZ) BLACK OLIVES, STONED

1 BOUQUET GARNI

PINCH OF SAFFRON POWDER

300 ML (½ PINT) DRY WHITE WINE

JUICE OF 1 LEMON

The chicken joints may be skinned if preferred. Season the flour, then coat the chicken joints in it. Heat the oil in a large oval cocotte. Add the joints and fry them for about 10 minutes or until they are golden brown all over. Remove the chicken from the cocotte and set aside. Lower the heat, add the onions and garlic, and cook these ingredients for 5 minutes. Stir in the tomatoes, olives, bouquet garni, saffron and wine, and bring to the boil.

Replace the chicken joints, cover the cocotte and simmer gently for 45 minutes or until the chicken joints are cooked through. Off the heat, discard the bouquet garni, then stir in the lemon juice. Taste and adjust the seasoning before serving.

Grillade de Poulet

MARINATED GRILLED CHICKEN

Marinating chicken before grilling ensures that it stays very moist, as well as giving it extra flavour.

SERVES 4–6

4–6 CHICKEN QUARTERS

MARINADE DE VIN BLANC (SEE PAGE 130)

150 ML (¼ PINT) CHICKEN STOCK

SALT AND FRESHLY MILLED BLACK PEPPER

TO GARNISH: FRESH BAY LEAVES

Wash and dry the chicken quarters. Make deep slashes into each one using a sharp knife. Place the chicken joints in a dish. Pour the marinade over them, cover and chill for at least 4 hours, or for up to 24 hours. Drain the chicken, reserving the marinade.

Heat a meat grill and place the chicken joints, skin-side down, on it. Cook for 20–30 minutes, turning several times, or until golden brown and cooked through. Pierce the joints in the thickest part to check that the meat is cooked: if there is any sign of blood in the juices, or pink meat, cook a little longer. Transfer the chicken to a heated serving dish, cover and keep hot.

Strain the reserved marinade into a small saucepan and add the stock. Bring to the boil, then boil rapidly until reduced by half. Taste and adjust the seasoning, then pour this sauce over the chicken. Garnish with bay leaves and serve.

Poulet Vallée d'Auge

CHICKEN WITH CIDER AND CALVADOS

Vallée d'Auge is one of the chief cider growing districts of Normandy and it is also an area that produces Calvados, the celebrated apple brandy. This recipe may be cooked in a marmitout, which is a multi-function casserole with a lid that can be used as a frying pan or skillet on the hob or under the grill.

SERVES 4

4 CHICKEN QUARTERS

SALT AND FRESHLY MILLED BLACK PEPPER

50 G (2 OZ) BUTTER

4 DESSERT APPLES

100 G (4 OZ) BUTTON MUSHROOMS, FINELY CHOPPED

300 ML (½ PINT) DRY CIDER

30 ML (2 TBSP) CALVADOS

150 ML (¼ PINT) DOUBLE CREAM

Skin the chicken joints, if preferred, then season them all over. Melt half the butter in a medium round casserole or marmitout. Add the chicken joints and fry quickly until they are golden brown on all sides.

Peel, core and finely chop two of the apples. Add the chopped apples to the chicken, cover the casserole and cook gently for 10 minutes. Put the mushrooms and cider in a small saucepan, bring to the boil, then simmer for 10 minutes. Pour the Calvados over the chicken and set it alight. When the flames have died down, strain the cider into the casserole, reserving the mushrooms. Cover the casserole and simmer the chicken very gently for about 30 minutes, or until the joints are cooked through.

Peel and core the remaining two apples, then cut them into rings. Heat the remaining butter in a small frying pan. Add the apple rings and fry them for about 5 minutes, turning several times, until they are golden brown.

Transfer the chicken to a heated serving dish, cover and keep hot. Boil the cooking liquor rapidly until it is reduced to about 150 ml (¼ pint). Stir in the cream and boil for a few minutes. Stir in the reserved mushrooms, cook for a further minute, then pour the sauce over the chicken. Garnish with fried apple rings and serve at once.

Poulet Farci aux Pruneaux

STUFFED ROAST CHICKEN WITH PRUNES

Agen in the Garonne is where the finest prunes in France are produced.

SERVES 6

1.8 KG (4 LB) CHICKEN, WITH GIBLETS

225 G (8 OZ) SAUSAGEMEAT

450 G (1 LB) TENDERISED PRUNES

25 G (1 OZ) RAISINS

2 SLICES OF WHITE BREAD

A LITTLE MILK

SALT AND FRESHLY MILLED BLACK PEPPER

1.25 ML (¼ TSP) GRATED NUTMEG

25 G (1 OZ) BUTTER

10 ML (2 TSP) CORNFLOUR, BLENDED WITH 30 ML (2TBSP) WATER

Reserve the chicken liver and heart from the giblets, finely chop them and mix them with the sausagemeat. Finely chop a few of the prunes, then add them to the sausagemeat with the raisins. Cut the crusts off the bread. Soak the bread in a little milk for 5 minutes, then wring it dry and add it to the sausagemeat. Season the mixture, add the nutmeg and mix well.

Rinse the chicken and pat dry. Loosely spoon the sausagemeat stuffing into the body cavity of the chicken, then truss the bird neatly.

Heat the butter in a large oval cocotte. Brown the chicken all over. Remove the cocotte from the heat and season the chicken. Cover and cook at 160°C (325°F) mark 3 for 3 hours. After 2 hours, add the remaining prunes to the liquid in the cocotte. Remove the lid for the last 30 minutes of cooking to brown.

Lift out the chicken and keep hot in a serving dish. Add 150 ml (¼ pint) water to the cooking liquor. Transfer the cocotte to the hob and thicken the sauce with the blended cornflour. Pour the sauce over the chicken.

Poulet au Riz

POT-ROASTED CHICKEN

Pot-roasting is a traditional country method of cooking slightly older birds to ensure their tenderness.

SERVES 6

100 G (4 OZ) LONG-GRAIN RICE

SALT AND FRESHLY MILLED BLACK PEPPER

50 G (2 OZ) RAISINS

2 CELERY STICKS, FINELY CHOPPED

25 G (1 OZ) BUTTER

1.8–2.3 KG (4–5 LB) CHICKEN, WITHOUT GIBLETS

225 G (8 OZ) BUTTON ONIONS, SKINNED

450 G (1 LB) SMALL TOMATOES, SKINNED

450 G (1 LB) CARROTS, PEELED AND QUARTERED, OR SMALL CARROTS, SCRAPED

60 ML (4 TBSP) WHITE WINE

Cook the rice in boiling salted water in a medium saucepan until tender – about 20 minutes. Drain the rice well. Stir in the raisins, celery and butter while the rice is still warm. Season well. Allow the mixture to cool before stuffing the chicken.

Rinse the chicken under cold water, flushing the body cavity under running water. Drain well, then pat the bird dry on absorbent kitchen paper. Cut off any lumps of fat. Loosely spoon the rice mixture into the body cavity of the chicken, then truss the bird neatly, tying the leg ends together and the wings close to the body.

Put the onions, tomatoes and carrots in a medium oval casserole and pour in the wine. Add some seasoning, then place the chicken on top of the vegetables and season the bird lightly. Cover the casserole and cook the chicken at 180°C (350°F) mark 4 for 2½ hours, or until it is cooked through. Serve the chicken with the vegetables and ladle the cooking juices over each portion.

POULET FARCI AUX PRUNEAUX

Poussins à l'Estragon

POUSSINS WITH TARRAGON

The combination of chicken and tarragon never fails to succeed.

SERVES 4

4 POUSSINS
1 LEMON, QUARTERED
6 TARRAGON SPRIGS
SALT AND FRESHLY MILLED BLACK PEPPER
25 G (1 OZ) BUTTER
30 ML (2 TBSP) PERNOD
150 ML (¼ PINT) DOUBLE CREAM

TO GARNISH: TARRAGON SPRIGS

Rinse the poussins under cold running water, then dry them on absorbent kitchen paper. Put a lemon quarter and a tarragon sprig inside each poussin, then season the birds all over. Place the poussins breast-side down in a large greased rectangular oven dish. Put a knob of butter and half a tarragon sprig on the back of each poussin, then roast the birds at 200°C (400°F) mark 6 for 25 minutes. Turn the poussins over so they are breast-side up and roast for a further 25 minutes or until they are cooked through.

Transfer the poussins to a heated serving plate, cover and keep hot. Place the oven dish on the hob and stir the Pernod and cream into the cooking juices. Bring to the boil, then boil rapidly until the sauce is reduced and thickened. Season to taste, then strain the sauce into a heated sauceboat. Garnish the poussins with tarragon sprigs and serve the sauce separately.

Caille au Genièvre

QUAIL COOKED WITH JUNIPER

A cassadou is a round shallow casserole. It is useful for sautés as well as casseroles and its lid fits on correspondingly sized skillets.

SERVES 4

100 G (4 OZ) BUTTER
8 QUAIL
SALT
300 ML (½ PINT) CHICKEN STOCK
6 JUNIPER BERRIES, WASHED
30 ML (2 TBSP) GIN OR BRANDY
WATERCRESS SPRIGS

Melt the butter in a cassadou and fry the birds until brown on all sides. Sprinkle with salt. Cover the pan and cook over moderate heat for about 20 minutes. If preferred, the birds can be cooked in the oven at 180°C (350°F) mark 4.

When the birds are nearly cooked, add the stock, juniper berries and gin or brandy. Continue to cook for a further 10 minutes until the birds are tender.

Remove the birds to a serving dish and keep hot. Transfer the cassadou to the hob, if necessary, and boil the liquor for 2–3 minutes to reduce it slightly. Spoon the sauce around the quail and garnish with watercress.

CANARD AUX NAVETS

DUCK WITH TURNIPS

It really is important to use small, young turnips for this – preferably freshly dug!

SERVES 4

1.8 KG (4 LB) DUCK, WITH GIBLETS

1 CARROT, PEELED AND QUARTERED

1 STICK CELERY, SLICED

2 ONIONS, 1 LARGE AND 1 SMALL, BOTH QUARTERED

SALT AND FRESHLY MILLED BLACK PEPPER

25 G (1 OZ) BUTTER

675 G (1½ LB) YOUNG TURNIPS, PEELED

15 ML (1 TBSP) SUGAR

1 BOUQUET GARNI

15 ML (1 TBSP) PLAIN FLOUR

Put the giblets from the duck in a medium saucepan. Add the carrot, celery and the small onion. Sprinkle in a little seasoning and pour in 1.1 litres (2 pints) water. Bring to the boil, cover and simmer for 1 hour. Strain the stock, then measure it. If necessary pour the stock back into the saucepan and boil it rapidly to reduce it to 900 ml (1½ pints).

Rinse the duck under cold water. Dry it on absorbent kitchen paper and discard any lumps of fat. Season the duck inside and out. Melt the butter in a large oval cocotte. Add the duck and cook it on all sides until it is golden brown. Remove the duck from the cocotte and set it aside.

Add the turnips and sugar to the butter remaining in the cocotte and cook for about 10 minutes or until the vegetables are golden. Pour in the giblet stock, add the bouquet garni and remaining large onion, and replace the duck in the cocotte. Cover and cook at 180°C (350°F) mark 4 for 1½ hours. Remove the lid of the cocotte and cook for a further 30–40 minutes, or until the duck skin is crisp.

Remove the duck and turnips from the casserole and arrange them on a heated serving dish. Cover and keep hot. Skim all the fat off the cooking liquor and remove the bouquet garni and onion. Reserve 15 ml (1 tbsp) of the fat. Put the cocotte over a high heat and boil the liquor rapidly until it is reduced by half. Blend the flour with the reserved duck fat and add to the liquor, a teaspoonful at a time, whisking well, until it is thickened and smooth. Taste the sauce and adjust the seasoning, then pour it into a heated sauceboat and serve it with the duck.

Overleaf: Left CANARD AUX NAVETS *(above)*, PIGEONS AUX PETITS POIS *(see page 77)*, PINTADE EN COCOTTE *(see page 77)*

Dindonneau Farci aux Marrons

TURKEY WITH CHESTNUT STUFFING

The finest French chestnuts come from the South West where they are also made into flour.

SERVES UP TO 15

450 G (1 LB) CHESTNUTS

150 ML (¼ PINT) TURKEY OR CHICKEN STOCK

1 BAY LEAF

1 THYME SPRIG

1 RASHER BACON, RINDED AND CHOPPED

1 CELERY STICK, CHOPPED

450 G (1 LB) GOOD-QUALITY PORK SAUSAGEMEAT

SALT AND FRESHLY MILLED BLACK PEPPER

1.25 ML (¼ TSP) GRATED NUTMEG

30 ML (2 TBSP) BRANDY

30 ML (2 TBSP) CHOPPED FRESH PARSLEY

1 EGG, LIGHTLY BEATEN

GRATED RIND OF ½ LEMON

4.5 KG (10 LB) TURKEY, WITHOUT GIBLETS

50 G (2 OZ) BUTTER

Peel the chestnuts by making a small slit in the top of each chestnut. Half fill a small saucepan with water, bring to the boil, add the chestnuts and cook for 5 minutes. Remove from the heat. Leave the chestnuts in the water and remove them one at a time and peel off the shell and the brown skin. Cut in half. Put the peeled chestnuts in a medium saucepan. Add the stock, bay leaf, thyme, bacon and celery, and bring to the boil. Cover the saucepan and simmer gently for 20 minutes, or until the chestnuts are soft. Discard the herbs, then purée the other ingredients in a blender or food processor. Leave the chestnut purée to cool. Mix the cooled purée with the sausagemeat, seasoning, nutmeg, brandy, parsley, beaten egg and lemon rind until thoroughly combined.

Rinse the turkey under cold water, flushing the body cavity thoroughly. Drain the bird well, then dry it with absorbent kitchen paper. Trim off any lumps of fat. Spoon the chestnut stuffing into the body cavity of the bird, then truss it neatly. Tie the legs ends together and the wings close to the body. Place the bird in a large rectangular oven dish. Spread the butter all over the turkey breast and season the bird all over. Cover the turkey with foil and roast it at 180°C (350°F) mark 4 for about 4 hours, or until it is cooked through. Baste the bird frequently during cooking and remove the foil for the last 45 minutes.

LAPIN À LA MOUTARDE

MUSTARD RABBIT

A popular way of cooking rabbit in the Sologne and other hunting areas.

SERVES 4

1 RABBIT, ABOUT 1.4 KG (3 LB) IN WEIGHT

300 ML (½ PINT) WHITE WINE

1 ONION, SKINNED AND CHOPPED

2 CARROTS, PEELED AND CHOPPED

A FEW PARSLEY STALKS

1 THYME SPRIG

2 CLOVES

SALT AND FRESHLY MILLED BLACK PEPPER

1 PIG'S TROTTER, SPLIT IN HALF

20 ML (4 TSP) FRENCH WHOLEGRAIN MUSTARD

100 G (4 OZ) SMOKED STREAKY BACON

The rabbit should be cleaned ready for cooking. Lay the rabbit in a large oval gratin dish. Pour in the wine, then add the onion, carrots, parsley stalks, thyme, cloves and seasoning. Cover and leave to marinate for 24 hours, turning the rabbit from time to time. Put the split trotter in a medium saucepan and pour in enough cold water to cover it. Bring to the boil, then turn off the heat and leave the trotter to soak for 5 minutes. Drain the trotter and remove the rabbit from the marinade. Strain the marinade and set it aside.

Dry the rabbit well with absorbent kitchen paper and spread the mustard all over it, both inside and out. Put the trotter inside the body cavity. Lay the bacon over the top of the rabbit and tie the bacon in place.

Place the rabbit in the gratin dish and roast it at 180°C (350°F) mark 4 for 1¼ hours, or until cooked through and tender. Remove the string and bacon, then discard the trotter. Carve the rabbit into portions: take a heavy meat knife and mallet or cleaver. Cut along the meat along the length of the rabbit, down the backbone. Cut across the rabbit to separate the hind quarters, using a mallet to push the knife through the bones. Chop these hindquarters in half to give two leg joints. Cut off the fore end of the rabbit in the same way, cutting the portion in half to give two joints. Cut the remaining saddle in half along its length, then across in two or three places to make neat portions. Transfer the portions to a heated serving dish, arranging them neatly and trimming away any bone ends. Cover and keep hot.

Add the strained marinade to the meat juices in the gratin dish, stir well and boil the mixture for 5 minutes. Pour this sauce into a heated sauceboat and serve it with the rabbit.

Canard aux Pêches

DUCK WITH PEACHES

Fresh peaches, poached in white wine, make a delightful addition to this dish.

SERVES 4

- 50 G (2 OZ) BUTTER
- 1 LARGE ONION, SKINNED AND SLICED
- 2 LARGE CARROTS, PEELED AND SLICED
- 4 BREASTS OF DUCK
- 2 LARGE TOMATOES, SKINNED AND SLICED
- SALT AND FRESHLY MILLED BLACK PEPPER
- 3 PEACHES (WHITE IF POSSIBLE)
- 300 ML (½ PINT) SWEET WHITE WINE
- 150 ML (¼ PINT) DUCK STOCK, MADE FROM GIBLETS
- 10 ML (2 TSP) CORNFLOUR OR POTATO FLOUR

Melt the butter in a large gratin dish. Add the onion and carrots and gently fry without browning. Remove the vegetables, draining well. Brown the duck breasts on all sides in the hot butter, then lift out. Drain off any remaining butter in the dish. Replace the vegetables with the sliced tomatoes on top. Put the duck on top of the vegetables and season well. Cook at 180°C (350°F) mark 4 for 45 minutes–1 hour, basting occasionally. Skin the peaches by plunging them into boiling water for 1 minute, then cold water for 1 minute. Halve them and remove the stones. Poach the peaches in the sweet white wine until tender. Leave to cool in the wine. Drain, but reserve the wine.

When the duck is cooked, lift out (it will be returned to the oven so it does not have to be kept hot). Carefully strain off all the fat and liquid from the vegetables, discard.

Put the cooked vegetables into a medium saucepan with the wine, stock and one of the peaches, chopped. Simmer for 10 minutes, then press through a sieve. Return the sauce to the pan, reheat and add the cornflour, blended with a little of the liquid. Cook, stirring until thickened. Taste and season. Put the duck breasts back into the gratin dish and pour over a little of the sauce to glaze them. Place the four peach halves around the duck and return to the oven for 15 minutes to reheat. Serve the remaining sauce separately.

CANARD AUX PÊCHES

LIÈVRE À L'AIL

HARE WITH GARLIC

Saddle of hare is often served with roasted garlic as there is a strong affinity between these two ingredients. Do not be put off by the quantity of garlic: during the long slow cooking, its flavour mellows to impart a very pleasant tang to the finished dish. If preferred, this recipe may be used for venison, substituting about a 1.4 kg (3 lb) leg of venison joint for the hare.

SERVES 8

- 1 HARE, ABOUT 2.3–2.7 KG (5–6 LB), JOINTED
- 600 ML (1 PINT) RED WINE
- JUICE OF 1 LEMON
- 90 ML (6 TBSP) OLIVE OIL
- 20 ML (4 TSP) CHOPPED FRESH OREGANO
- SALT AND FRESHLY MILLED BLACK PEPPER
- 25 G (1 OZ) PLAIN FLOUR
- 1 LARGE ONION, SKINNED AND CHOPPED
- 1 HEAD OF GARLIC, SEPARATED, SKINNED AND CHOPPED
- 8 JUNIPER BERRIES, CRUSHED
- 150 ML (¼ PINT) CHICKEN STOCK
- 15 ML (1 TBSP) SOFT BROWN SUGAR

TO GARNISH: 45 ML (3 TBSP) CHOPPED FRESH PARSLEY
GRATED RIND OF 1 LEMON

Place the hare joints in a large oval gratin dish. Mix the wine, lemon juice, 30 ml (2 tbsp) olive oil, 15 ml (1 tbsp) oregano and seasoning. Pour this mixture over the hare, cover and leave to marinate in the refrigerator for 1–2 days. Turn and baste the joints with the marinade from time to time. Remove the hare joints from the marinade, drain and dry them on absorbent kitchen paper, then toss them in the flour.

Heat the remaining oil in a large cocotte. Add the hare joints and fry them quickly until they are browned on all sides. Remove the joints from the pan and set aside. Lower the heat, add the onion and garlic, and cook gently for 10 minutes. Stir in any remaining marinade, the juniper berries, remaining oregano, stock and sugar. Bring to the boil, then replace the hare joints and cover the cocotte. Simmer the hare gently for 3 hours or until the meat is very tender. Taste the sauce and adjust the seasoning before serving. Mix the parsley with the lemon rind and sprinkle this mixture over the hare joints. Serve at once.

Pintade en Cocotte

BRAISED GUINEA FOWL WITH CELERY

Guinea fowl can be a little dry but braising them, especially if using a doufeu, ensures that they remain moist and succulent. A doufeu is a large casserole with a specially shaped lid into which water or ice is placed during cooking. As a result the lid remains cool and allows moisture to continually baste the food. This method is particularly good for drier meats such as guinea fowl or veal.

SERVES 6

2 GUINEA FOWL

3 HEADS OF CELERY, TRIMMED AND HALVED LENGTHWAYS

15 ML (1 TBSP) OLIVE OIL

25 G (1 OZ) BUTTER

15 ML (1 TBSP) CHOPPED FRESH MARJORAM

150 ML (¼ PINT) DRY WHITE WINE

150 ML (¼ PINT) CHICKEN STOCK

SALT AND FRESHLY MILLED BLACK PEPPER

Rinse the guinea fowl under cold running water, then drain and dry them on absorbent kitchen paper. Make sure that the celery is perfectly clean and free of grit.

Heat the oil and butter in a large oval cocotte or doufeu. Add the guinea fowl and fry them quickly until they are golden brown all over. Remove the birds from the cocotte and set them aside. Add the celery to the pan, placing the halves cut side down, and fry quickly until golden brown. Pour in the wine and stock, and add some seasoning. Bring to the boil, then replace the guinea fowl on top of the celery. Cover the cocotte and simmer gently for 2–2½ hours or until the guinea fowl are tender. Transfer the birds to a heated serving dish and arrange the celery around them; cover and keep hot.

Boil the cooking liquor rapidly until it is reduced to 300 ml (½ pint), then taste it and adjust the seasoning. Pour the liquor into a heated sauceboat and serve with the birds.

Pigeons aux Petits Pois

PIGEONS WITH PETITS POIS AND BASIL

As with many other casseroles, especially game ones, the flavour of this dish is improved if it is made the day before and then reheated. In this case, reheat for 45 minutes, then add the peas and ham and cook for 15 minutes.

SERVES 4

4 PIGEONS

45 ML (3 TBSP) HAZELNUT OR OLIVE OIL

1 LARGE ONION, SKINNED AND CHOPPED

300 ML (½ PINT) DRY WHITE WINE

15 ML (1 TBSP) CHOPPED FRESH BASIL

SALT AND FRESHLY MILLED BLACK PEPPER

450 G (1 LB) FROZEN PETITS POIS

225 G (8 OZ) COOKED HAM, CHOPPED

Rinse the pigeons in cold water, then dry them with absorbent kitchen paper. Heat 30 ml (2 tbsp) of the oil in a large cocotte. Add the pigeons and fry them quickly until browned on all sides. Remove the pigeons from the pan and set aside.

Add the remaining oil to the pan, heat it gently, then add the onion and cook it gently for 5 minutes. Pour in the wine, basil and seasoning, and bring to the boil.

Replace the pigeons in the cocotte, cover and cook at 160°C (325°F) mark 3 for 2 hours, or until the pigeons are very tender.

Fifteen minutes before the end of cooking, add the peas and ham to the cocotte and stir gently. Taste and adjust the seasoning.

Faisan aux Poivrons

PHEASANT AND PEPPER CASSEROLE

Roasting is the most popular method of cooking young pheasants, but for birds of an uncertain age, casseroling ensures that they arrive at the table tender.

SERVES 6

60 ML (4 TBSP) OLIVE OIL

2 PHEASANTS, HALVED OR JOINTED

1 LARGE ONION, SKINNED AND CHOPPED

3 GARLIC CLOVES, CRUSHED

2 RED PEPPERS, SEEDED AND SLICED

1 GREEN OR YELLOW PEPPER, SEEDED AND SLICED

450 G (1 LB) TOMATOES, SKINNED AND CHOPPED

5 ML (1 TSP) CHOPPED FRESH ROSEMARY

SALT AND FRESHLY MILLED BLACK PEPPER

5 ML (1 TSP) CORNFLOUR

Heat 30 ml (2 tbsp) of the oil in a large oval cocotte. Add the pieces of pheasant and fry them quickly until golden brown all over. Remove from the cocotte and set aside.

Add the remaining oil to the cocotte and heat it gently. Add the onion and garlic and cook gently for 5 minutes. Add the pepper and cook for a further 5 minutes. Stir in the tomatoes, rosemary and seasoning, and bring to the boil. Replace the pheasant pieces in the cocotte.

Cover the cocotte and cook the pheasant at 160°C (325°F) mark 3 for 2–3 hours or until the meat is very tender. Lift out the pheasant and keep hot. Transfer the cocotte to the hob and stir in the cornflour, blended with a little cold water. Bring to the boil, then taste and adjust the seasoning of the sauce before serving.

Perdrix au Chou

CASSEROLED PARTRIDGE WITH CABBAGE

An old farmhouse way of cooking partridges.

SERVES 4

1 LARGE SAVOY CABBAGE

SALT AND FRESHLY MILLED BLACK PEPPER

30 ML (2 TBSP) OLIVE OIL

2 PARTRIDGES, HALVED

225 G (8 OZ) LEAN STREAKY BACON, IN ONE PIECE, RINDED AND CUT INTO 2 CM (¾ INCH) CUBES

2 LARGE CARROTS, PEELED AND CHOPPED

1 BOUQUET GARNI

2 GARLIC CLOVES, CRUSHED

4 SMOKED SAUSAGES, SUCH AS CHORIZO

300 ML (½ PINT) CHICKEN STOCK

Roughly chop the cabbage and cook it in a large saucepan of boiling salted water for about 8 minutes. Drain the cabbage well.

Heat the oil in a large oval cocotte. Add the halved partridges and cook them until golden brown on all sides. Remove the partridges from the pan and set aside. Add the bacon to the fat remaining in the pan and cook it for 5 minutes. Use a draining spoon to remove the bacon and take the pan off the heat.

Put half the cabbage in the base of the cocotte. Add the partridges, the bacon cubes, carrots, bouquet garni, garlic, sausages and seasoning, then top with the remaining cabbage. Pour in the stock, cover the cocotte and cook at 160°C (325°F) mark 3 for about 2½ hours, or until the partridges are tender. Taste and adjust the seasoning before serving.

Beef, Lamb, Pork and Veal

Rumsteck à la Crème et aux Chanterelles

RUMP STEAK WITH CREAM AND CHANTERELLES

Chanterelle mushrooms, or girolles as they are also known, give added flavour to this dish. However, if they are unavailable, oyster mushrooms can be substituted very satisfactorily.

SERVES 4

4 RUMP STEAKS, ABOUT 225 G (8 OZ) EACH

SALT

5 ML (1 TSP) CRUSHED GREEN PEPPERCORNS

50 G (2 OZ) BUTTER

10 ML (2 TSP) OLIVE OIL

100 G (4 OZ) CHANTERELLES, THINLY SLICED, OR OYSTER MUSHROOMS

30 ML (2 TBSP) RED WINE VINEGAR

150 ML (¼ PINT) DOUBLE CREAM

30 ML (2 TBSP) CHOPPED FRESH PARSLEY

Season the steaks with salt and the crushed green peppercorns. Heat the butter and oil in a large frying pan. Add the steaks and fry them on both sides: the cooking time depends on how well done you like your steaks, about 3 minutes each side gives a medium-rare steak. Transfer the steaks to a heated serving dish and keep hot. Add the chanterelles to the juices remaining in the pan and cook them gently for 3–4 minutes. Add the vinegar and quickly bring the juices to the boil. Reduce the heat before stirring in the cream and parsley, then heat gently without allowing the cream to boil. Taste and adjust the seasoning, then pour the mushrooms and sauce over the steaks. Serve at once.

Pot-au-Feu

BOILED BEEF

There are many regional and family versions of this recipe. This one comes from Séverina's kitchen at Le Creuset.

SERVES 6

900 G (2 LB) LEAN BEEF, SUCH AS SILVERSIDE, TOPSIDE OR CHUCK

450 G (1 LB) OXTAIL, CUT INTO 4 PIECES

2 SMALL ONIONS, SKINNED

4 CLOVES

2 MEDIUM CARROTS, PEELED AND CUT INTO CHUNKS

2 LEEKS, WHITE PARTS ONLY, TRIMMED

1 SMALL TURNIP, PEELED AND CUT INTO LARGE CHUNKS

2 CELERY STICKS, CUT INTO LARGE PIECES

1 BOUQUET GARNI, CONSISTING OF 1 BAY LEAF, FEW PARSLEY STALKS, FEW THYME SPRIGS, CELERY LEAVES

SALT AND FRESHLY MILLED BLACK PEPPER

ACCOMPANYING VEGETABLES

450 G (1 LB) SMALL POTATOES, PEELED AND LEFT WHOLE

1 MEDIUM FIRM CABBAGE, CUT INTO QUARTERS

Put the beef joint into a large cocotte with the oxtail, cover with cold water and bring to the boil. Carefully remove all the scum as the water boils. Add the onions, studded with the cloves, the carrots, leeks, turnip, celery and bouquet garni, season well. Cover and simmer for about 3 hours.

When cooked, remove the cover and allow several hours to cool so that the fat rises to the surface and can be skimmed off.

To serve, cook the potatoes and cabbage in a large saucepan of boiling salted water for 10 minutes. Strain and re-cover with some of the stock from the beef. Cook until tender. Reheat the beef thoroughly in the stock. Serve thickly sliced with the vegetables.

Boeuf à la Mode de Caen

BEEF WITH VEGETABLES AND CIDER

This is a marvellous dish which can be left in the oven, quite forgotten, for several hours. It is typical of many other dishes which were once taken by locals to the village baker's oven to be cooked in the residual heat following the morning's baking. The casserole was always sealed with a flour and water paste to ensure that none of the steam escaped; however the close fitting lids of Le Creuset pans makes this quite unnecessary in this recipe. The calf's foot in this dish is not essential but does enrich the flavour.

SERVES 6

1 CALF'S FOOT

25 G (1 OZ) BUTTER

15 ML (1 TBSP) OIL

1.1 KG (2½ LB) BONED AND ROLLED BRISKET

30 ML (2 TBSP) CALVADOS

1.1 LITRES (2 PINTS) CIDER

A FEW BEEF BONES, CHOPPED INTO PIECES (OPTIONAL)

450 G (1 LB) BUTTON ONIONS, SKINNED

450 G (1 LB) SMALL CARROTS, PEELED OR SCRAPED

2 GARLIC CLOVES, CRUSHED

10 ML (2 TSP) FRENCH MUSTARD

SALT AND FRESHLY MILLED BLACK PEPPER

1 BOUQUET GARNI

Ask the butcher to split the calf's foot for you. Put it into a medium saucepan and cover with cold water. Bring to the boil and cook the foot for 5 minutes, then drain it. Heat the butter and oil in a medium casserole. Add the beef and cook it quickly on all sides to seal it. Pour the Calvados over the joint and set it alight. When the flames have died down, pour in the cider. Put the beef bones in the casserole (if used), then add the onions, carrots, garlic, mustard, seasoning and bouquet garni. Put the calf's foot in the casserole, cover and cook at 140°C (275°F) mark 1 for 4 hours.

Remove the calf's foot from the pan, cut all the meat off it and chop this roughly, discarding the skin. Place the chopped meat on a heated serving dish with the beef, carrots and onions. Cover and keep hot. Discard the bones and bouquet garni. Skim the fat off the cooking liquor and boil it rapidly until it is reduced by about half. Taste and adjust the seasoning, then pour the reduced liquor into a sauceboat and serve it with the meat and vegetables.

Filets de Boeuf au Fromage

FILLET STEAK TOPPED WITH CHEESE

Cooking the steaks for 3 minutes on each side will produce a rare steak. Increase the cooking time as desired.

SERVES 4

SALT AND FRESHLY MILLED BLACK PEPPER

4 FILLET STEAKS, ABOUT 2 CM (¾ INCH) THICK

10 ML (2 TSP) CHOPPED FRESH THYME

15 ML (1 TBSP) OLIVE OIL

4 THIN SLICES GOAT'S CHEESE, ABOUT 0.5 CM (¼ INCH) THICK AND 7.5 CM (3 INCHES) WIDE, OR USE ROQUEFORT

Season the steaks and sprinkle the thyme over them. Brush a little olive oil over a meat grill, then place it over a moderate heat. When the grill is hot, place the steaks on it and cook them for about 3 minutes on each side. Pour off and reserve any juices from the grill and keep them hot.

Place a slice of cheese on each steak, then put them under a hot grill for about 2 minutes, or until the cheese is bubbling. Transfer the steaks to a heated serving dish and pour over the reserved meat juices. Serve immediately.

Boeuf en Daube

BEEF CASSEROLE

SERVES 6

2 ONIONS, SKINNED AND SLICED

2 CARROTS, PEELED AND SLICED

2 GARLIC CLOVES, CRUSHED

1 BAY LEAF

1 ROSEMARY SPRIG

3 PARSLEY SPRIGS

2 CLOVES

6 BLACK PEPPERCORNS

5 ML (1 TSP) SALT

PARED RIND OF ½ AN ORANGE

15 ML (1 TBSP) RED WINE VINEGAR

450 ML (¾ PINT) RED WINE

1.1 KG (2½ LB) LEAN BRAISING STEAK, CUT INTO 5 CM (2 INCH) CUBES

2 RASHERS SMOKED STREAKY OR FLANK BACON, RINDED AND DICED

15 ML (1 TBSP) OLIVE OIL

25 G (1 OZ) PLAIN FLOUR

100 G (4 OZ) GREEN OR BLACK OLIVES, OR A MIXTURE OF BOTH

Put the onions, carrots, garlic, herbs, cloves, peppercorns, salt, orange rind, vinegar and wine into a medium round or oval cocotte. Add the beef to the ingredients in the cocotte. Mix well, cover and leave for 24 hours.

Drain the meat and reserve the marinade. Rinse out the cocotte. Put the bacon in the cocotte with the olive oil and heat it gently until the fat runs from the bacon. Increase the heat and add the meat. Cook, stirring, until the meat is browned on all sides.

Sprinkle the flour into the pan and cook stirring until the contents are lightly browned. Strain the marinade, then add it to the meat mixture with 150 ml (¼ pint) water, stirring all the time. Bring to the boil. Cover the cocotte and cook at 150°C (300°F) mark 2 for about 3 hours, until the meat is tender. Stone the olives and add halfway through cooking. Season before serving.

Top BOEUF EN DAUBE, *Left* CÔTES DE PORC AUX POIVRONS *(see page 88)*

Veau aux Tomates

VEAL WITH TOMATOES AND MUSHROOMS

SERVES 4

25 G (1 OZ) BUTTER

15 ML (1 TBSP) OLIVE OIL

4 SHALLOTS, SKINNED AND CHOPPED

1 GARLIC CLOVE, CRUSHED

675 G (1½ LB) STEWING VEAL, CUT INTO 2.5 CM (1 INCH) CUBES

25 G (1 OZ) PLAIN FLOUR

150 ML (¼ PINT) DRY WHITE WINE

300 ML (½ PINT) VEAL OR CHICKEN STOCK

15 ML (1 TBSP) CHOPPED FRESH OREGANO

4 TOMATOES, SKINNED, QUARTERED AND SEEDED

SALT AND FRESHLY MILLED BLACK PEPPER

175 G (6 OZ) BUTTON MUSHROOMS

25 G (1 OZ) BLACK OLIVES

Heat the butter and oil in a medium round cocotte. Add the shallots, garlic and meat and cook these ingredients together for about 10 minutes. Stir in the flour and cook for a further 2 minutes, stirring frequently. Pour in the wine and stock, and bring to the boil, stirring all the time. Add the oregano, tomatoes and seasoning, then cover the pan and simmer the veal gently for 1¼–1½ hours or until it is tender. Stir occasionally during cooking.

Stir in the mushrooms and olives, and continue cooking for a further 10–15 minutes. Taste and adjust the seasoning before serving.

Escalopes de Veau au Vermouth

VEAL ESCALOPES WITH VERMOUTH

The flavour of the vermouth used in this recipe complements the fennel.

SERVES 4

SALT AND FRESHLY MILLED BLACK PEPPER

4 ESCALOPES OF VEAL, BEATEN OUT THINLY

15 ML (1 TBSP) LEMON JUICE

50 G (2 OZ) BUTTER

15 ML (1 TBSP) OLIVE OIL

1 SMALL BULB OF FENNEL, FINELY CHOPPED

75 ML (5 TBSP) DRY WHITE VERMOUTH

150 ML (¼ PINT) DOUBLE CREAM

Season the meat and sprinkle the lemon juice over the escalopes. Heat the butter in a large frying pan with the oil. Add the escalopes and fry them on both sides until they are beginning to brown. Transfer to a heated serving dish and keep hot.

Add the fennel to the fat remaining in the frying pan and cook gently for 5 minutes. Pour in the vermouth and bring to the boil, then lower the heat before stirring in the cream. Heat through gently, taste and adjust the seasoning, then pour the fennel sauce over the escalopes and serve at once.

Veau Braisé
BRAISED VEAL

One of the simplest methods of braising veal so that it retains all its natural flavour.

SERVES 4–6

40 G (1½ OZ) BUTTER
1–1.4 KG (2–3 LB) VEAL JOINT
225 G (8 OZ) BUTTON ONIONS, SKINNED
4 CELERY STICKS, CHOPPED
1 TARRAGON SPRIG
SALT AND FRESHLY MILLED BLACK PEPPER
350 G (12 OZ) CARROTS, PEELED AND SLICED
PINCH OF SUGAR

Melt half the butter in a doufeu (see page 77). Add the veal and fry until it is browned all over, turning frequently. Stir in the onions, celery, tarragon and seasoning. Pour in 300 ml (½ pint) water, then heat gently until the water is simmering.

Cover and simmer the veal very gently for about 3 hours, or until it is tender. Stir from time to time during cooking. Taste and adjust the seasoning before serving.

Prepare the carrots to serve with the braised veal. Place them in a medium saucepan. Add the sugar and pour in enough water to half cover the vegetables. Add the butter and bring to the boil. Cook the carrots for about 15–20 minutes, until they are tender. The water should have evaporated leaving the vegetables coated in a buttery glaze.

Veau Braisé au Chablis
POT-ROASTED VEAL WITH CHABLIS SAUCE

It may sound extravagant to use a fine wine, such as a Chablis, for cooking, but the end result justifies the extra expenditure.

SERVES 6

25 G (1 OZ) BUTTER
3 ONIONS, SKINNED AND QUARTERED
4 CARROTS, PEELED AND CHOPPED
1 TOMATO, QUARTERED
1 THYME SPRIG
1 SMALL BAY LEAF
1 GARLIC CLOVE, CRUSHED
SALT AND FRESHLY MILLED BLACK PEPPER
1.1 KG (2½ LB) LOIN OR BEST END OF VEAL, BONED AND ROLLED, BONES CHOPPED UP AND RESERVED
150 ML (¼ PINT) VEAL OR CHICKEN STOCK
300 ML (½ PINT) CHABLIS OR OTHER DRY WHITE WINE

Melt the butter in a large oval cocotte. Add the onions, carrots, tomato, thyme, bay leaf and garlic, and cook for about 10 minutes. Season the mixture, add the veal bones, then place the joint in the cocotte and pour in the veal or chicken stock. Cover the cocotte and put it in the oven at 150°C (300°F) mark 2 for 2½ hours. Baste the meat from time to time during cooking. Remove the meat from the cocotte, place it on a heated serving dish, cover and keep hot. Add the Chablis to the casserole, bring the sauce to the boil on the hob and boil it rapidly until it is reduced by half. Strain the sauce into a heated sauceboat and serve this sauce with the veal.

Gigot d'Agneau Farci

STUFFED LEG OF LAMB

SERVES 8

350 G (12 OZ) SALT PORK

1 LARGE SLICE OF BREAD

A LITTLE MILK

3 TOMATOES, SKINNED, SEEDED AND CHOPPED

15 ML (1 TBSP) CHOPPED FRESH PARSLEY

5 ML (1 TSP) CHOPPED FRESH ROSEMARY

15 ML (1 TBSP) CHOPPED FRESH CHIVES

3 GARLIC CLOVES, CRUSHED

SALT AND FRESHLY MILLED BLACK PEPPER

1 EGG YOLK

1.8–2.3 KG (4–5 LB) LEG OF LAMB, BONED

60 ML (4 TBSP) OLIVE OIL

1 ONION, SKINNED AND CHOPPED

4 CARROTS, PEELED AND CHOPPED

2 TURNIPS, PEELED AND CHOPPED

1 CELERY STICK, CHOPPED

300 ML (½ PINT) DRY WHITE WINE

1 BOUQUET GARNI

Soak the pork in cold water to cover for at least 4 hours. Drain the meat, remove any skin and bones, and mince the meat finely. Cut the crusts off the bread, place it in a dish and soak in a little milk. Leave for 5 minutes, then wring the bread completely dry. Mix the minced pork with the bread, tomatoes, herbs, garlic and seasoning. Bind with the egg yolk. Use this mixture to stuff the lamb, then tie the joint in a neat shape with string.

Heat the oil in a large rectangular oven dish. Add the lamb and brown the joint all over, then remove it from the pan. Add the onion, carrots, turnips and celery to the fat in the dish and cook, stirring often, until golden brown. Pour in the wine and replace the meat in the dish. Add a little seasoning and the bouquet garni. Bake at 160°C (325°F) mark 3 for 2½ hours, basting once or twice during cooking. If all the liquid evaporates during cooking, add about 150 ml (¼ pint) water to keep the vegetables moist.

GIGOT D'AGNEAU FARCI, RATATOUILLE *(see page 116)*

ÉPAULE D'AGNEAU AUX NOIX

SHOULDER OF LAMB STUFFED WITH NUTS AND ORANGE

This dish looks very attractive if, after it has been sewn to enclose the stuffing, it is made into a round 'ballotine'. To do this, take the trussing needle up to the centre each time, dividing the meat effectively into eight sections.

SERVES 6

25 G (1 OZ) BUTTER

1 SMALL ONION, SKINNED AND VERY FINELY CHOPPED

225 G (8 OZ) GOOD-QUALITY PORK SAUSAGEMEAT OR MINCED PORK

50 G (2 OZ) SHELLED WALNUTS, VERY FINELY CHOPPED OR GROUND

50 G (2 OZ) PINE NUTS, ROUGHLY CHOPPED

5 ML (1 TSP) CHOPPED FRESH ROSEMARY

GRATED RIND OF 2 ORANGES

SALT AND FRESHLY MILLED BLACK PEPPER

1.4 KG (3 LB) SHOULDER OF LAMB, BONED

JUICE OF 2 ORANGES

Melt the butter in a small saucepan. Add the onion and fry it for 5 minutes. Mix the cooked onion with the sausagemeat or pork, walnuts, pine nuts, rosemary, orange rind and seasoning.

Lay the meat out on a board and fill the cavity left by the bone with the stuffing. Using coarse thread or fine string and a trussing needle, sew up the joint, neatly to enclose the stuffing completely.

Place the meat in a small rectangular oven dish and season. Roast the lamb at 220°C (425°F) mark 7 for 20 minutes, then reduce the oven temperature to 180°C (350°F) mark 4 and cook the meat for a further 1 hour 30 minutes, or until cooked through.

Add 30 ml (2 tbsp) water to the orange juice and use this to baste the meat half way through cooking.

Transfer the cooked meat to a heated serving dish. Skim off all the fat from the cooking juices, then strain them into a heated sauceboat. Remove the string from the lamb and carve it into thick slices; serve the sauce separately.

CÔTES DE PORC AUX POIVRONS

PORK CHOPS WITH PEPPERS

There is a tendency for today's leaner pork to be slightly dry, but the juices from the peppers together with the tomatoes and wine, keeps it moist.

SERVES 4

45 ML (3 TBSP) OLIVE OIL

4 PORK CHOPS

SALT AND FRESHLY MILLED BLACK PEPPER

1 MEDIUM ONION, SKINNED AND CHOPPED

1 GARLIC CLOVE, CRUSHED

2 GREEN PEPPERS, SEEDED AND SLICED

2 RED PEPPERS, SEEDED AND SLICED

225 G (8 OZ) TOMATOES, SKINNED AND CHOPPED

45 ML (3 TBSP) WHITE WINE

5 ML (1 TSP) CHOPPED FRESH SAGE

Heat the oil in a medium round cocotte. Season the chops and put them in the cocotte. Fry the chops quickly on both sides until browned. Remove from the cocotte and set aside.

Add the onion and garlic to the oil remaining in the cocotte and cook gently for 5 minutes. Add the peppers and continue to cook gently for a further 10 minutes. Stir in the tomatoes, wine and sage, and add a little seasoning. Replace the chops in the cocotte, cover and cook gently for 20 minutes or until the chops are very tender. Taste the cooking juices and adjust the seasoning before serving.

Longe d'Agneau à la Moutarde

ROAST LOIN OF LAMB WITH MUSTARD AND VINEGAR

This recipe comes from Orléans, where for centuries they have been justly proud of both their vinegar and mustard.

SERVES 6–8

SALT AND FRESHLY MILLED BLACK PEPPER

1.8 KG (4 LB) LOIN OF LAMB

30 ML (2 TBSP) MOUTARDE D'ORLÉANS OR OTHER MILD FRENCH MUSTARD

15 ML (1 TBSP) ORLÉANS WHITE WINE VINEGAR OR OTHER WHITE WINE VINEGAR

300 ML (½ PINT) MUSCADET OR OTHER DRY WHITE WINE

Season the lamb well, then spread the mustard all over the joint. Place the lamb in a large rectangular oven dish and roast it at 190°C (375°F) mark 5 for 1½ hours. Baste the meat with its juices from time to time during cooking.

When the meat is cooked, transfer it to a heated serving dish, cover and keep hot. Skim all the fat off the juices in the cooking dish. Place the dish on the hob, add the vinegar and wine, and bring to the boil. Simmer the sauce for about 5 minutes. Taste and adjust the seasoning, then serve this sauce with the lamb.

Agneau aux Pommes de Terres

LAMB WITH POTATOES AND CARROTS

A recipe from the Languedoc which was often used for cooking mutton.

SERVES 2

2 LAMB STEAKS, ABOUT 1.5 CM (½ INCH) THICK

100 G (4 OZ) STREAKY BACON, RINDED AND CUT INTO THIN STRIPS

2 GARLIC CLOVES, CUT INTO FINE SLIVERS

30 ML (2 TBSP) OLIVE OIL

450 G (1 LB) POTATOES, PEELED AND CUT INTO 5 CM (2 INCH) CHUNKS

2 CARROTS, PEELED AND ROUGHLY CHOPPED

1 MARJORAM SPRIG

SALT AND FRESHLY MILLED BLACK PEPPER

250 ML (8 FL OZ) LAMB OR CHICKEN STOCK

Make small holes through the lamb steaks with the point of a skewer. Trim the bacon strips to about 5 cm (2 inches) in length. Thread the bacon and garlic through the holes in the meat. If you have a larding needle, use it for the bacon. Place the meat in a cassadou with any remaining bacon and garlic, and the oil. Add the potatoes, carrots and marjoram to the cocotte. Sprinkle seasoning over the ingredients and pour in the stock.

Put the cassadou, uncovered, in the oven at 220°C (425°F) mark 7 and cook for 10 minutes. Cover the cassadou, lower the oven temperature to 150°C (300°F) mark 2 and cook for a further 3 hours. At the end of cooking the meat will be very tender and the stock will have been absorbed by the vegetables.

Côtes de porc Campagnardes

MARINATED PORK CHOPS WITH HERBS

SERVES 4

150 ML (¼ PINT) RED WINE

30 ML (2 TBSP) RED WINE VINEGAR

1 CARROT, PEELED AND CHOPPED

1 SMALL ONION, SKINNED AND CHOPPED

1 SHALLOT, SKINNED AND CHOPPED

1 GARLIC CLOVE, CRUSHED

1 BAY LEAF

A FEW PARSLEY STALKS

1 THYME SPRIG

3 BLACK PEPPERCORNS

3 JUNIPER BERRIES

5 ML (1 TSP) SALT

4 THICK PORK CHOPS

25 G (1 OZ) BUTTER

15 ML (1 TBSP) OLIVE OIL

150 ML (¼ PINT) CHICKEN STOCK

15 ML (1 TBSP) REDCURRANT OR GERANIUM LEAF JELLY

Pour the wine and vinegar into a small saucepan. Add the carrot, onion, shallot, garlic, bay leaf, parsley stalks, thyme, peppercorns, juniper berries and salt. Bring slowly to the boil and simmer for 2–3 minutes, then leave to cool.

Place the chops in a large gratin dish and pour the cooled marinade mixture over them. Cover and chill in the refrigerator for about 2 days, turning the chops several times.

Drain the chops, reserving the marinade, and pat them dry on absorbent kitchen paper. Heat the butter and oil in a large frying pan. Add the chops and fry them for about 5 minutes on each side, or until they are golden brown.

Strain the marinade and pour it over the chops. Pour in the stock and heat until simmering. Cook the chops gently for about 20 minutes, uncovered, or until they are quite tender.

Transfer the chops to a heated serving dish, cover and keep hot. Add the jelly to the sauce in the pan and cook, stirring, for 2–3 minutes. Taste and adjust the seasoning, then pour the sauce over the chops and serve at once.

Filet de Porc en Croûte

FILLET OF PORK IN PUFF PASTRY

SERVES 6–8

25 G (1 OZ) BUTTER

5 SHALLOTS, SKINNED AND CHOPPED

100 G (4 OZ) FIRM MUSHROOMS, CHOPPED

GRATED RIND OF 1 LEMON

JUICE OF ½ LEMON

60 ML (4 TBSP) FRESH WHITE BREADCRUMBS

15 ML (1 TBSP) CHOPPED FRESH PARSLEY

SALT AND FRESHLY MILLED BLACK PEPPER

900 G (2 LB) PORK FILLET, CUT INTO EQUAL SIZED PIECES

450 G (1 LB) PUFF PASTRY

1 EGG, BEATEN

Heat the butter in a frying pan. Add the shallots and lightly fry without browning. Stir in the mushrooms and cook until they are softened. Add the lemon rind, juice, breadcrumbs, parsley and seasoning. Cook until all the juices have been absorbed. Cool. Slice each piece of fillet through lengthwise so that it can be opened out. Beat with a rolling pin to flatten slightly. Spread with the cooled stuffing, then fold into original shape. Roll out the pastry into a large oblong about 50×18 cm (20×7 inches). Cut in half so that each piece measures 25×18 cm (10×7 inches). (If using frozen puff pastry, thaw thoroughly before using.) Place a fillet on the pastry, brush the edges of the pastry with egg and form into a parcel with the join underneath and the ends securely sealed. Decorate the top with pastry leaves, then make two steam vents. Brush the pastry with beaten egg and transfer to a well greased small rectangular oven dish.

Bake at 200°C (400°F) mark 6 for about 50 minutes–1 hour. If pastry is browning reduce heat slightly for last 10 minutes.

CÔTES DE PORC CAMPAGNARDES

Foie de Veau en Papillote

CALF'S LIVER IN PAPER

SERVES 4

- 50 G (2 OZ) LONG-GRAIN RICE
- 150 ML (¼ PINT) VEAL OR CHICKEN STOCK
- 25 G (1 OZ) UNSALTED BUTTER, MELTED
- OUTER LEAVES OF 1 LETTUCE
- SALT AND FRESHLY MILLED BLACK PEPPER
- 4 SLICES CALF'S LIVER, THINLY SLICED
- 8 SAGE LEAVES
- 45 ML (3 TBSP) MADEIRA OR PORT

Put the rice in a medium saucepan and pour in the stock. Bring to the boil. Cover and simmer very gently for about 20 minutes or until the rice is tender and all the stock has been absorbed.

Take four large pieces of greaseproof paper. Fold them in half, cut out half an oval, measuring about 30 cm (12 inches) at its widest, from each piece of paper. Open out the ovals, place them on the work surface and brush with the melted butter.

Lay 4–5 lettuce leaves on each oval of paper. Sprinkle with a little seasoning, then neaten the edges of the lettuce leaves, trimming them so that there is a 2.5 cm (1 inch) border of paper free all around the edge.

Divide the rice between the packs, spreading it over the middle. Season the slices of liver and arrange them neatly on top of the rice. Add 2 sage leaves to each parcel. Pour 10 ml (2 tsp) Madeira or port over each parcel, them carefully fold the sides of the paper up to enclose the filling. The package should now take the same shape as the orginal half-oval. Pleat the paper together around the edge, leaving a small hole at one end.

Insert a drinking straw into the hole and blow air into the package, then remove the straw and pleat the paper together to seal in the air. Repeat with the remaining packages.

Place an oven dish in the oven at 220°C (425°F) mark 7 for 5 minutes. Brush the dish with a little oil. Place the greaseproof packages in the dish, return to the oven and cook for 8 minutes; do not overcook.

Slit the packages open and serve.

Blanquette de Veau

BLANQUETTE OF VEAL

SERVES 6

- 50 G (2 OZ) BUTTER
- 900 G (2 LB) STEWING VEAL, CUT INTO CUBES
- 15 ML (1 TBSP) PLAIN FLOUR
- 1.1 LITRES (2 PINTS) VEAL STOCK OR WATER
- 2 CARROTS, PEELED AND THINLY SLICED
- 1 MEDIUM ONION, SKINNED AND CHOPPED
- 1 GARLIC CLOVE, CRUSHED
- 1 BOUQUET GARNI
- SALT AND FRESHLY MILLED BLACK PEPPER
- 225 G (8 OZ) BUTTON MUSHROOMS, THICKLY SLICED
- 2 EGG YOLKS
- JUICE OF 1 LEMON
- 60 ML (4 TBSP) DOUBLE CREAM

Heat the butter in a large cocotte. Add the pieces of veal and fry until lightly browned. Add the flour and stir well to absorb all the juices. Gradually pour in the stock, stirring, then add the vegetables, bouquet garni and seasoning. Cover and cook at 180°C (350°F) mark 4 for 1½ hours, or until the veal is tender. Add the mushrooms for the last 30 minutes. Remove the veal and vegetables to a heated serving dish and keep hot.

Strain the sauce through a sieve into a medium saucepan. Beat together the egg yolks, lemon juice and cream. Add slowly to the sauce, whisking all the time. Heat gently, without boiling, until the sauce thickens. Adjust seasoning, then pour over the veal.

Foie de Veau aux Chanterelles

CALF'S LIVER WITH CHANTERELLES

Calf's liver should always be cooked very simply, as in this recipe, so that its delicate flavour is not overwhelmed.

SERVES 4

A LITTLE PLAIN FLOUR

SALT AND FRESHLY MILLED BLACK PEPPER

450 G (1 LB) CALF'S LIVER, THINLY SLICED

25 G (1 OZ) BUTTER

15 ML (1 TBSP) OLIVE OIL

175 G (6 OZ) CHANTERELLES OR BUTTON MUSHROOMS, FINELY CHOPPED

15 ML (1 TBSP) CHOPPED FRESH PARSLEY

15 ML (1 TBSP) CHOPPED FRESH CHIVES

1 GARLIC CLOVE, CRUSHED

15 ML (1 TBSP) LEMON JUICE

Sprinkle some flour on a plate and season it well. Dust the liver with this flour. Heat the butter and oil in a large frying pan. Add the liver and cook the slices for 3 minutes on each side. Transfer the liver to a heated serving dish, cover and keep hot.

Add the mushrooms to the fat remaining in the pan. Stir in the herbs, garlic and lemon juice, then cook for a further 5 minutes, stirring frequently. Spoon the mushroom mixture over the liver and serve at once.

Rognons de Veau aux Genièvres

VEAL KIDNEYS WITH JUNIPER BERRIES

This recipe from north-eastern France is also popular in Belgium.

SERVES 4

4 VEAL KIDNEYS, SKINNED AND CORED

50 G (2 OZ) BUTTER

45 ML (3 TBSP) DRY WHITE WINE

SALT AND FRESHLY MILLED BLACK PEPPER

12 JUNIPER BERRIES, CRUSHED

Cut the kidneys into thin slices. Melt the butter in a large oval cocotte or cassadou (see page 68). Add the kidneys and fry them quickly on both sides. Pour in the wine, then add the seasoning and juniper berries. Cover and simmer very gently for a further 10 minutes or until the kidneys are cooked through. Taste and adjust the seasoning, then serve at once.

TOURTE BOURGUIGNONNE

PORK AND VEAL PIE

A Le Creuset gratin dish makes the perfect container for this pie as the cast iron ensures a crisp base.

SERVES 4

- 225 G (8 OZ) LEAN MINCED PORK
- 225 G (8 OZ) LEAN MINCED VEAL
- 1 MEDIUM ONION, SKINNED AND VERY FINELY CHOPPED
- 1 GARLIC CLOVE, CRUSHED
- 30 ML (2 TBSP) CHOPPED FRESH PARSLEY
- 5 ML (1 TSP) CHOPPED FRESH THYME
- PINCH OF GRATED NUTMEG
- SALT AND FRESHLY MILLED BLACK PEPPER
- 15 ML (1 TBSP) BRANDY
- 1 QUANTITY PÂTE BRISÉE (SEE PAGE 156)
- 1 EGG, SEPARATED

Mix the pork, veal, onion, garlic, parsley, thyme, nutmeg and seasoning. When thoroughly combined, mix in the brandy. Divide the pastry in half. Roll the pieces into two circles; one about 23 cm (9 inches) in diameter, the other 18 cm (7 inches) in diameter. Lightly butter an 18 cm (7 inch) gratin dish and line it with the larger circle of pastry. Brush the egg white all over the pastry to prevent the meat juices from soaking through it. Beat the egg yolk with 10 ml (2 tsp) water.

Spoon the meat into the pastry case and pack it down well. Brush the edges of the pastry with a little egg yolk. Lift the second circle of pastry over the filling, then seal, trim and flute the edges. Make two or three small cuts on the top of the pastry to allow steam to escape during cooking. Brush with egg. Bake at 200°C (400°F) mark 6 for 10 minutes, then reduce the oven temperature to 180°C (350°F) mark 4 and bake the pie for a further 40 minutes. Serve hot.

ESCALOPE FARCIE AU JAMBON

ESCALOPE OF VEAL WITH HAM STUFFING

A light veal dish where the sauce is delicately flavoured with fromage frais.

SERVES 4

- 4 ESCALOPES OF VEAL
- 75 G (3 OZ) FRESH WHITE BREADCRUMBS
- 100 G (4 OZ) HAM, FINELY CHOPPED
- 5 ML (1 TSP) CHOPPED FRESH SAGE
- SALT AND FRESHLY MILLED BLACK PEPPER
- 1 EGG, BEATEN
- 25 G (1 OZ) BUTTER FOR FRYING
- 300 ML (½ PINT) WHITE STOCK
- 25 G (1 OZ) BUTTER
- 25 G (1 OZ) PLAIN FLOUR
- 60 ML (4 TBSP) FROMAGE FRAIS

Beat the escalopes until quite thin. Mix together the breadcrumbs, ham, sage, seasoning and egg. Divide the stuffing between the escalopes, spreading it all over the meat. Roll up and secure with pieces of string.

Melt the butter in a medium cocotte. Add the pieces of meat and gently fry until browned all over. Remove from the heat, then add the stock and a little seasoning. Cover and cook at 180°C (350°F) mark 4 for about 1–1¼ hours, or until the meat is tender.

Remove the escalopes to serving dish, remove the string and keep hot. Blend the butter and flour together until smooth to make a beurre manié. Put the cocotte over a low heat and stir in small pieces of the beurre manié. Stir until thickened. Remove from the heat and stir in the fromage frais. Check the seasoning, then pour the sauce over the escalopes.

TOURTE BOURGUIGNONNE

Chou Farci

STUFFED CABBAGE

A staple recipe from the South West, this dish has the most superb flavour.

SERVES 6

1 LARGE CRISP SAVOY CABBAGE

SALT AND FRESHLY MILLED BLACK PEPPER

15 G (½ OZ) BUTTER

100 G (4 OZ) SMOKED STREAKY BACON, RINDED AND CHOPPED

2 LARGE ONIONS, SKINNED AND CHOPPED

2 GARLIC CLOVES, CRUSHED

350 G (12 OZ) GOOD-QUALITY PORK SAUSAGEMEAT OR LEAN MINCED PORK

100 G (4 OZ) COOKED LONG-GRAIN RICE

225 G (8 OZ) TOMATOES, SKINNED AND CHOPPED

225 G (8 OZ) COOKED SPINACH, FINELY CHOPPED

1 CELERY STICK, FINELY CHOPPED

30 ML (2 TBSP) CHOPPED FRESH PARSLEY

5 ML (1 TSP) FINELY CHOPPED FRESH THYME

300 ML (½ PINT) CHICKEN STOCK

2 CARROTS, PEELED AND CHOPPED

2 LEEKS, TRIMMED AND CHOPPED

Half fill a large round cocotte with water, add a teaspoon of salt and bring to the boil. Leave the cabbage whole, but remove about five of the large outer leaves. Wash both thoroughly. Add the cabbage and the separate leaves to the boiling water, and cook for 4 minutes. Drain the vegetables and rinse in cold water, then drain again, placing the cabbage upside down in a colander so that all the water runs from between the leaves.

Melt the butter in a small saucepan. Add the bacon, one of the onions and the garlic, and cook for about 8 minutes or until golden brown. Thoroughly mix the cooked ingredients with the sausagemeat or pork, rice, tomatoes, spinach, celery, herbs and plenty of seasoning.

Very carefully open out the cabbage, leaf by leaf. Starting in the centre, spoon some of the stuffing between each leaf. Wrap the large leaves around the outside of the cabbage and tie it securely with string. Pour the stock into the cocotte and add the remaining onion, the carrots and leeks. Put the cabbage in the cocotte, cover and cook at 160°C (325°F) mark 3 for 3 hours.

Carefully lift the cabbage from the cocotte, remove the string and discard the outer leaves used to wrap the cabbage.

FONDUES

Fondue Bourguignonne

MEAT FONDUE

Possibly the most popular fondue of all, it is important to use good quality steak for this meal. Never overfill the fondue pan with oil and always take great care when cooking at the table. Remember not to eat the meat straight off the fondue fork – it must be slipped off the fondue fork on to a plate and eaten with a cold fork.

SERVES 6

900 G (2 LB) GOOD-QUALITY RUMP STEAK OR FILLET STEAK

6 PARSLEY OR BASIL SPRIGS

FONDUE SAUCES (SEE PAGE 99)

450 ML (¾ PINT) VEGETABLE OR SUNFLOWER OIL

30 ML (2 TBSP) HUILE AUX HERBES (SEE PAGE 129), OPTIONAL

Cut the meat into 2.5 cm (1 inch) cubes and arrange it on six individual serving plates. Cover and chill until ready to eat. Garnish with parsley or basil.

Prepare a selection of sauces and place them on the table. Pour the oils into the fondue pan. Put the oil on the hob over moderate heat until a cube of bread added to the pan browns in about 1 minute.

Light the spirit stove at the table and carefully take the pan of oil to it.

Each person spears the meat cubes on the fondue forks and cooks them in the hot oil. The sauces are eaten with the cooked meat. Serve warm, crusty French bread or potatoes and a green salad with the fondue.

Fondue de Viande à la Savoyarde

SAVOIE MEAT FONDUE

This is similar to a fondue Bourguignonne but a selection of different meats is offered as well as steak: bacon rolls, little sausages, pork and chicken may be included. Unlike steak, which can be served rare, these ingredients must be cooked through in the hot oil.

Sauces pour Fondues

FONDUE SAUCES

Serve several different sauces with a meat fondue – about four or six are the usual number. Mayonnaise (see page 125), Aïoli (see page 124), Sauce rémoulade (see page 124) and Sauce tartare (see page 125) are some of the classic sauces to serve. Here are two popular sauces that take only minutes to make.

Devilled Tomato Sauce

60 ML (4 TBSP) SOURED CREAM

10 ML (2 TSP) TOMATO PURÉE

2.5 ML (½ TSP) SUGAR

2.5 ML (½ TSP) CHILLI SAUCE

5 ML (1 TSP) MILD MUSTARD

SALT AND FRESHLY MILLED BLACK PEPPER

Mix all the ingredients. Taste and adjust the seasoning before serving.

Curry Sauce

15 ML (1 TBSP) MILD CURRY POWDER OR CURRY PASTE

15 ML (1 TBSP) CHUTNEY

75 ML (5 TBSP) MAYONNAISE

Mix all the ingredients together in a bowl.

Sauces pour Fondue à la Moutarde, aux Tomates et aux Anchois

MUSTARD, TOMATO AND ANCHOVY FONDUE SAUCES

One basic sauce is turned into three very different fondue sauces.

SERVES 4–6

150 ML (¼ PINT) OLIVE OIL

450 ML (¾ PINT) NUT OIL

4 EGG YOLKS

30 ML (2 TBSP) WHITE WINE VINEGAR

JUICE OF 1 LEMON

SALT

CAYENNE

5 ML (1 TSP) DIJON MUSTARD

2.5 ML (½ TSP) PIMENTO OIL

15 ML (1 TBSP) TOMATO PURÉE

2.5 ML (½ TSP) TABASCO SAUCE

6 CANNED ANCHOVY FILLETS, IN OIL

1 HARD-BOILED EGG YOLK

To make the basic sauce, heat the oils in large saucepan over a moderate heat to 45°C (115°F). Meanwhile mix the egg yolks together and put in a double saucepan over a very gentle heat. Beat in the vinegar and add half the lemon juice. Carefully mix in the hot oil, a little at a time, stirring briskly. If the sauce becomes too thick, then add some of the remaining lemon juice. Season with salt and cayenne.

Divide the basic sauce into three. To one sauce add the Dijon mustard and pimento oil.

To the second sauce, mix in the tomato purée and tabasco sauce. For the remaining sauce, crush the anchovies with the hard-boiled egg yolk and add a pinch of cayenne. Mix into the sauce.

Fondue aux Champignons

MUSHROOM FONDUE

A delicious creamy fondue which is lighter than cheese fondue.

SERVES 4

1 FRENCH LOAF

25 G (1 OZ) BUTTER

2 SHALLOTS, SKINNED AND FINELY CHOPPED

225 G (8 OZ) BUTTON MUSHROOMS, FINELY CHOPPED

5 ML (1 TSP) CHOPPED FRESH THYME

300 ML (½ PINT) DOUBLE CREAM

15 ML (1 TBSP) CHOPPED FRESH PARSLEY

50 G (2 OZ) GRUYÈRE CHEESE, FINELY GRATED

30 ML (2 TBSP) PERNOD

SALT AND FRESHLY MILLED BLACK PEPPER

Cut the bread into bite-sized cubes. Place them in a large gratin dish and put them in the oven at 130°C (250°F) mark ½ for about 30 minutes, or until the bread has dried out a little.

Melt the butter in the fondue pan. Add the shallots and cook them gently for 3–4 minutes. Add the mushrooms and thyme, then cook for 5 minutes, stirring frequently.

Pour in the cream, bring the mixture to the boil and continue to boil until the fondue is thick and creamy, stirring frequently. Stir in the parsley, cheese and Pernod, then heat gently for a further 2–3 minutes, or until the cheese has melted. Taste and adjust the seasoning.

Light the spirit stove at the table and put the pan on it. Serve with the cubes of bread which are dipped into the mushroom fondue, using forks.

Fondue aux Trois Fromages

FONDUE WITH THREE CHEESES

This is a very rich fondue, using Comté, Gruyère and Beaufort.

SERVES 6

1 LARGE FRENCH LOAF

225 G (8 OZ) COMTÈ

225 G (8 OZ) GRUYÈRE

175 G (6 OZ) BEAUFORT

300 ML (½ PINT) DRY WHITE WINE

50 G (2 OZ) BUTTER

15 ML (1 TBSP) POTATO FLOUR

PINCH OF GRATED NUTMEG

FRESHLY MILLED BLACK PEPPER

30 ML (2 TBSP) COGNAC

Cut the bread into bite-sized cubes. Place them in a large gratin dish and put them in the oven at 130°C (250°F) mark ½ for about 30 minutes, or until the bread has dried out a little.

Thinly slice all the cheese. Reserve 45 ml (3 tbsp) of the wine and pour the remainder into the cheese fondue pan. Add the butter and bring to the boil on the hob. Turn the heat to the lowest setting and gradually whisk in the cheese. Make sure each addition has melted before adding more cheese. When all the cheese has been incorporated blend the reserved wine with the potato flour and stir this into the fondue. Season with nutmeg and pepper, and stir in the Cognac.

Light the spirit burner at the table. Put the pot of fondue over the burner. Serve with the bread cubes which are dipped into the fondue, using forks.

Fondue aux Oeufs

CHEESE AND EGG FONDUE

Brillat Savarin's fondue is, in fact, creamy scrambled egg with cheese rather than a cheese fondue in the Swiss sense. It is important to cook it slowly so that it remains creamy and does not become too firm and solid.

SERVES 4

- 1 FRENCH LOAF
- 6 EGGS
- 100 G (4 OZ) GRUYÈRE CHEESE, FINELY GRATED
- 50 G (2 OZ) BUTTER, CUT INTO SMALL PIECES
- SALT AND FRESHLY MILLED BLACK PEPPER

Cut the bread into bite-sized cubes. Place them in a large gratin dish and put them in the oven at 130°C (250°F) mark ½ for about 30 minutes, or until the bread has dried out a little. Beat the eggs and tip them into a cheese fondue pan. Stir in the cheese and butter. Beat in the seasoning, then beat well to ensure all the ingredients are combined.

Light the spirit stove at the table and put the pan on it. Cook the egg mixture very gently, stirring all the time, until it thickens. The bread may be skewered and dipped into the fondue, or a little fondue may be spooned out on to plates and eaten with a fork, accompanied by the bread.

Fondue Savoyarde

CHEESE FONDUE

For best results, use a third each of the Gruyère, Emmenthal and Comté.

SERVES 4–6

- 1 LARGE FRENCH LOAF
- 1 GARLIC CLOVE, HALVED
- 600 ML (1 PINT) DRY WHITE WINE
- 175 G (6 OZ) CHEESE PER PERSON SUCH AS GRUYÈRE, EMMENTHAL OR COMTÉ, CUBED
- 15 ML (1 TBSP) CORNFLOUR
- 30 ML (2 TBSP) KIRSCH

Cut the bread into bite-sized cubes. Place them in a large gratin dish and put them in the oven at 130°C (250°F) mark ½ for about 30 minutes, or until the bread has dried out a little.

Rub the garlic all over the inside of a cheese fondue pan. Reserving about 45 ml (3 tbsp) of the wine, pour the remainder into the pan. Bring the wine to the boil on the hob. Turn the heat to the lowest setting and gradually stir in the cubes of cheese. (It is essential that the heat is maintained on a very low setting and that each addition of cheese is melted before the next is added.) When all the cheese has been incorporated, blend the reserved wine with the cornflour and stir into the fondue. Add the kirsch and cook for 5 minutes.

Light the spirit stove at the table and put the pan of cheese fondue over it. The bread cubes are speared on fondue forks and dipped in the fondue. The fondue will be very hot, therefore care should be taken especially if children are dipping into it.

Fondue aux Fruits de Mer

SEAFOOD FONDUE

Many fish or shellfish can be used but a selection of three or four varieties makes it more interesting. Cod, John Dory, monkfish, sole, large prawns or scampi are all firm fish and ideal to use.

SERVES 4–6

450 ML (¾ PINT) COOKING OIL

THINLY PARED RIND 1 LEMON

FEW PARSLEY SPRIGS

FEW MARJORAM SPRIGS

2 BAY LEAVES

SELECTION OF FISH, ALLOWING 175 G (6 OZ) PER PERSON

Pour the oil into the fondue pan, add the lemon rind and herbs and leave to infuse for 2–3 hours.

Cut the fish into bite sized pieces, dry well and arrange on serving plates.

Put the fondue pan on the hob over a moderate heat and heat until a cube of bread added to the pan browns in 1 minute. Light the spirit stove at the table and carefully take the pan of oil to it.

Each person spears the fish on a fondue fork and cooks it in the oil until lightly browned. Serve a selection of well flavoured sauces, such as Tartare (see page 125), Devilled Tomato (see page 99), Curry (see page 99) and Anchovy (see page 105).

Fondue au Chocolat du Lait et à l'Orange

CHOCOLATE AND ORANGE FONDUE

This chocolate fondue is likely to appeal to children.

SERVES 6

200 G (7 OZ) MILK CHOCOLATE, BROKEN INTO PIECES

GRATED RIND OF 1 ORANGE

150 ML (¼ PINT) SINGLE CREAM

FOR DIPPING: APPROXIMATELY 900 G (2 LB) PREPARED FRESH FRUIT (SEE FONDUE AU CHOCOLAT PAGE 102), SQUARES OF CAKE, SPONGE FINGERS

Place the chocolate, orange rind and cream in a chocolate fondue pan. Place the pan over a very low heat on the hob until the chocolate melts, stirring frequently.

Light the spirit stove at the table. Put the pan on the spirit stove over a very gentle heat. Use the fondue forks to skewer fruit or pieces of cake and dip them into the fondue. Sponge fingers may be dipped by skewering them on forks.

FONDUE SAVOYARDE *(see page 101)*

FONDUE AU CHOCOLAT

RICH CHOCOLATE FONDUE

Squares of cake or sponge fingers and fresh fruit may be dipped into chocolate fondue, according to taste. A variety of fresh fruit may be served: cubes of pineapple, strawberries, apple slices, peach slices, pear slices, orange or tangerine segments.

SERVES 6

- 225 G (8 OZ) PLAIN CHOCOLATE, BROKEN INTO PIECES
- 150 ML (¼ PINT) DOUBLE CREAM
- 22.5 ML (4½ TSP) RUM, BRANDY OR LIQUEUR (FOR EXAMPLE, TIA MARIA, GRAND MARNIER OR COINTREAU
- 40 G (1½ OZ) BLANCHED ALMONDS, FINELY CHOPPED

FOR DIPPING: ABOUT 900 G (2 LB) FRESH FRUIT, PREPARED ACCORDING TO TYPE, SQUARES OF CAKE, SPONGE FINGERS

Put the chocolate and cream into a chocolate fondue pan. Place over a low heat on the hob until the chocolate melts, stirring frequently. Stir in the rum, brandy or liqueur and the nuts.

Light the spirit stove at the table. Put the pan on the stove over very gentle heat. Use the fondue forks to skewer the fruit or cake and dip the pieces into the fondue. Sponge fingers may be dipped without forks.

FONDUE AUX ABRICOTS

APRICOT FONDUE

Not all sweet fondues need be rich with chocolate or cream. This version can be made with plums as well as apricots and has a refreshing flavour at the end of a meal.

- 450 G (1 LB) FRESH APRICOTS
- 100 G (4 OZ) SUGAR
- FINELY GRATED RIND AND JUICE OF 1 LARGE ORANGE
- 300 ML (½ PINT) WATER
- 30 ML (2 TBSP) APRICOT BRANDY
- 5-10 ML (1–2 TSP) CORNFLOUR

TO DIP: MARSHMALLOWS, SPONGE FINGERS, CHUNKS OF BANANA, SLICES OF APPLE OR PEAR.

Cut the apricots in half and remove the stones. Put the apricots, sugar, orange rind and juice into the fondue pot with the water. Simmer on the hob for 30–40 minutes or until the apricots are very tender. Cool slightly then transfer to an electric blender and liquidise until smooth. Return to the fondue pot, add the brandy and cornflour blended with a little water. (The amount of cornflour needed will vary depending on how much juice the apricots produced.) Cook on the hob until thickened.

Light the spirit stove at the table and transfer the fondue pot to it.

Using fondue forks dip marshmallows, sponge fingers and firm fruits into the sauce.

Bagna Cauda

HOT ANCHOVY DIP

Whilst the asparagus and artichokes are cooling after cooking, prepare the remaining vegetables for dipping.

SERVES 6

225 G (8 OZ) ASPARAGUS, TRIMMED AND COOKED

3 GLOBE ARTICHOKES, TRIMMED AND COOKED

4 CARROTS, PEELED

6 CELERY STICKS

3 COURGETTES, TRIMMED

1 BUNCH RADISHES, TRIMMED

1 SMALL CAULIFLOWER, BROKEN INTO FLORETS

1 LARGE RED PEPPER, SEEDED AND CUT INTO STRIPS

1 LARGE GREEN PEPPER, SEEDED AND CUT INTO STRIPS

DIP

150 ML (¼ PINT) OLIVE OIL

75 G (3 OZ) BUTTER

2 GARLIC CLOVES, FINELY CHOPPED

TWO 50 G (2 OZ) CANS ANCHOVY FILLETS, DRAINED AND FINELY CHOPPED

Cool the asparagus and artichokes. Cut the carrots, celery and courgettes into finger-sized sticks.

Heat the oil and butter in a fondue pan until just melted, but not foaming. Add the garlic and cook gently for 2 minutes. Do not allow it to colour. Add the anchovies and cook very gently, stirring all the time, for 10 minutes or until the anchovies dissolve into a paste. Dip the vegetables into the hot anchovy sauce.

Fondue au Bleu

BLUE CHEESE FONDUE

Roquefort cheese, reputed to be the finest blue cheese in the world, is ripened in caves at Cambalon, a small area south of the Massif Central.

SERVES 6

1 GARLIC CLOVE, HALVED

600 ML (1 PINT) DRY WHITE WINE

450 G (1 LB) GRUYÈRE CHEESE, GRATED

225 G (8 OZ) BLEU DE BRESSE OR ROQUEFORT CHEESE, CRUMBLED

10 ML (2 TSP) CORNFLOUR OR POTATO FLOUR

FRESHLY MILLED BLACK PEPPER

A LITTLE GRATED NUTMEG

A LITTLE SALT (IF NECESSARY)

Rub the inside of a cheese fondue pan thoroughly with the cut clove of garlic. Add the wine to the pan, reserving 10 ml (2 tsp), and heat slowly on the hob until it begins to bubble. Add the cheeses, a little at a time, stirring continuously. Mix the cornflour with the reserved wine and stir into the fondue. Add seasonings but taste before adding salt.

Light the spirit stove at the table and put the pan of cheese fondue over it. Serve with cubes of French bread (see page 100).

ORANGE
CERISES
Sirop
D'ANANAS
ABRICOTS

Vegetables and Salads

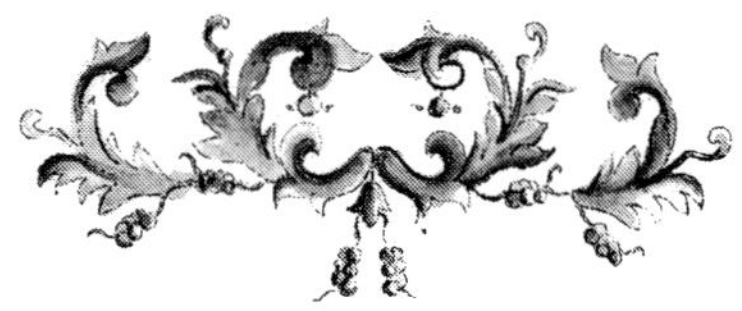

Tian à la Provençale

AUBERGINE GRATIN

Salting, or dégorging, aubergines draws out excess moisture and removes any bitter-tasting juices.

SERVES 4

450 G (1 LB) AUBERGINES

SALT AND FRESHLY MILLED BLACK PEPPER

25 G (1 OZ) BUTTER

25 G (1 OZ) PLAIN FLOUR

300 ML (½ PINT) MILK

60 ML (4 TBSP) FRESHLY GRATED PARMESAN CHEESE

1.25 ML (¼ TSP) GRATED NUTMEG

ABOUT 150 ML (¼ PINT) OLIVE OR VEGETABLE OIL

350 G (12 OZ) TOMATOES, SKINNED AND SLICED

2 GARLIC CLOVES, ROUGHLY CHOPPED

2 EGGS, BEATEN

Slice the aubergines thinly, then place in a colander, sprinkling each layer with salt. Cover with a plate, place heavy weights on top and leave to dégorge for 30 minutes. Meanwhile, melt the butter in a saucepan. Add the flour and cook gently, stirring, for 1–2 minutes. Remove from the heat and gradually blend in the milk. Bring to the boil, stirring constantly, then simmer for 3 minutes until thick and smooth. Add half of the cheese, the nutmeg and seasoning to taste, stir well to mix, then remove from the heat.

Rinse the aubergine slices under cold running water, then pat dry with absorbent kitchen paper. Pour enough oil into a heavy-based frying pan to cover the base. Heat until very hot, then add a layer of aubergine slices. Fry over moderate heat until golden brown on both sides, turning once. Remove with a slotted spoon and drain on absorbent kitchen paper. Repeat with more oil and aubergines. Arrange alternate layers of aubergines and tomatoes in an oiled large gratin dish. Sprinkle each layer with garlic, a little salt and plenty of pepper. Beat the eggs into the sauce, then pour slowly into the dish. Sprinkle the remaining cheese evenly over the top. Bake at 200°C (400°F) mark 6 for 20 minutes, or until golden brown and bubbling. Serve hot.

Gratin de Pommes de Terre et Courgettes

GRATIN OF POTATOES AND COURGETTES

SERVES 6

900 G (2 LB) WAXY POTATOES, PEELED

450 G (1 LB) COURGETTES

BUTTER, FOR GREASING

1 GARLIC CLOVE, CRUSHED

SALT AND FRESHLY MILLED BLACK PEPPER

15 ML (1 TBSP) CHOPPED FRESH THYME

300 ML (½ PINT) DOUBLE CREAM

25 G (1 OZ) BUTTER, CUT INTO SMALL PIECES

Cut the potatoes and courgettes into 0.5 cm (¼ inch) thick slices. Cook the potatoes in a saucepan of boiling salted water for 3 minutes, adding the courgettes to the pan for the last minute. Drain.

Put half the vegetables in a well buttered gratin dish, add half the garlic and some seasoning. Add the remaining vegetables, garlic and a little more seasoning. Beat the thyme and cream together and pour evenly over the vegetables. Dot the top with the pieces of butter.

Cook at 180°C (350°F) mark 4 for 30–40 minutes, or until the vegetables are tender.

Céleri-rave à la Sauce Tomate

CELERIAC WITH TOMATO SAUCE

When in good condition, celeriac should be firm and heavy for its size. If light in weight, the flesh will be airy and spongy.

SERVES 4–6

2 HEADS OF CELERIAC, TOTAL WEIGHT ABOUT 900 G (2 LB)

5 ML (1 TSP) LEMON JUICE

50 G (2 OZ) BROWN OR WHITE BREADCRUMBS

50 G (2 OZ) PARMESAN CHEESE, FRESHLY GRATED

TOMATO SAUCE

60 ML (4 TBSP) OLIVE OIL

1 LARGE ONION, SKINNED AND FINELY CHOPPED

3 GARLIC CLOVES, CRUSHED

350 G (12 OZ) RIPE TOMATOES, SKINNED AND FINELY CHOPPED

15 ML (1 TBSP) TOMATO PURÉE

30 ML (2 TBSP) RED WINE OR RED WINE VINEGAR

60 ML (4 TBSP) CHOPPED FRESH PARSLEY

5 ML (1 TSP) GROUND CINNAMON

1 BAY LEAF

SALT AND FRESHLY MILLED BLACK PEPPER

To make the tomato sauce, heat the oil in a heavy-based saucepan. Add the onion and garlic and fry gently for about 10 minutes until very soft and lightly coloured. Add the tomatoes, tomato purée, wine, parsley, cinnamon, bay leaf and seasoning to taste. Add 450 ml (¾ pint) hot water and bring to the boil, stirring with a wooden spoon to break up the tomatoes. Lower the heat, cover and simmer the tomato sauce for 30 minutes, stirring occasionally.

Meanwhile, peel the celeriac, then cut into chunky pieces. As you prepare the celeriac, place the pieces in a bowl of water to which the lemon juice has been added, to prevent discolouration. Drain the celeriac, then plunge quickly into a large pan of boiling salted water. Return to the boil and blanch for 10 minutes. Drain the celeriac well, then put into a large gratin dish. Pour over the tomato sauce (discarding the bay leaf) and sprinkle the breadcrumbs and cheese evenly over the top.

Bake at 190°C (375°F) mark 5 for 30 minutes, or until the celeriac is tender when pierced with a skewer and the topping is golden brown. Serve hot, straight from the dish.

Échalotes au Beurre

GLAZED SHALLOTS

Shallots are smaller than onions and have a milder flavour. They keep well, so it is worth buying a supply when you see them. Store them in a cool, dry place and use them up as soon as they show any signs of sprouting.

SERVES 4

450 G (1 LB) SHALLOTS, SKINNED

40 G (1½ OZ) BUTTER

SALT AND FRESHLY MILLED BLACK PEPPER

TO GARNISH: CHOPPED FRESH PARSLEY

Put the shallots in a marmitout and cover with water. Bring to the boil and cook, covered, for 10 minutes. Drain well.

Melt the butter in the marmitout skillet. Add the shallots and sauté for about 8–10 minutes until tender and well glazed. Season to taste. Transfer the shallots to a heated serving dish and sprinkle with the parsley.

Asperges à la Sauce Mousseline

ASPARAGUS WITH MOUSSELINE SAUCE

Asparagus is one of the most delicious of all vegetables. To prepare, scrape or shave the length of each stalk, starting just below the tip. Trim the stalks to roughly the same length.

SERVES 6

900 G (2 LB) FRESH ASPARAGUS, TRIMMED

SAUCE

3 EGG YOLKS

15 ML (1 TBSP) LEMON JUICE

A LITTLE SALT

FRESHLY MILLED WHITE PEPPER

175 G (6 OZ) BUTTER, CUT INTO SMALL PIECES

60 ML (4 TBSP) DOUBLE CREAM

Steam the asparagus spears in a steamer over a cocotte for 10–15 minutes until tender. Keep hot in a serving dish.

To make the sauce, beat the egg yolks, lemon juice and seasoning in a basin. Add a piece of butter and beat again. Stand the basin over a pan of hot water and whisk the yolks until thick and creamy. Remove from the heat but leave the basin over the hot water. Gradually beat in the remaining butter until the sauce is thick. Whip the cream and fold into the sauce just before serving over the asparagus.

Carottes et Champignons au Beurre

CARROTS AND MUSHROOMS IN BUTTER

If possible, select the new sweet baby carrots, sold complete with their greenery, available in bunches in early summer.

SERVES 4–6

25 G (1 OZ) BUTTER

450 G (1 LB) YOUNG CARROTS, SCRUBBED AND THICKLY SLICED

2 SHALLOTS, SKINNED AND CHOPPED

150 ML (¼ PINT) CHICKEN STOCK

SALT AND FRESHLY MILLED BLACK PEPPER

450 G (1 LB) BUTTON MUSHROOMS

10 ML (2 TSP) CHOPPED FRESH PARSLEY

A LITTLE GRATED NUTMEG

Melt the butter in a medium saucepan. Add the carrots and shallots and sauté for 3–4 minutes without colouring. Add the stock, salt and a little pepper. Cover and cook over a low heat for 15 minutes.

Add the mushrooms, parsley and nutmeg, cover and cook for a few minutes, until the mushrooms are tender. Remove the vegetables to a heated serving dish and keep hot. Simmer the remaining stock until reduced to about 30 ml (2 tbsp). Spoon over the carrots and mushrooms.

Petites Mousses aux Poireaux

LEEK MOUSSES

Delicious and impressive looking, these pale green mousses go well with fish dishes, or can be served as a starter or light lunch dish on their own. Because leeks harbour dirt it is best to slice them before washing thoroughly in a colander.

SERVES 8

- 450 G (1 LB) LEEKS, TRIMMED AND THINLY SLICED
- SALT AND FRESHLY MILLED BLACK PEPPER
- 25 G (1 OZ) BUTTER
- 30 ML (2 TBSP) PLAIN FLOUR
- 300 ML (½ PINT) MILK
- 150 G (5 OZ) SOFT CHEESE WITH GARLIC AND HERBS
- 2 EGGS
- 25 G (1 OZ) FRESH BROWN OR WHITE BREADCRUMBS

Place the leeks in a medium saucepan of boiling salted water and cook for about 5 minutes until tender. Drain well and rinse with cold water.

Meanwhile, put the butter, the flour and milk in a medium saucepan. Heat, whisking continuously, until the sauce thickens, boils and is smooth. Simmer for 2–3 minutes. Add half the cooked leeks and leave to cool.

Place the cooled sauce, soft cheese, eggs and breadcrumbs in a blender or food processor and process until almost smooth. Season.

Lightly grease eight 100 ml (4 fl oz) ramekin dishes and scatter a few of the reserved leeks in the bottom of each. Carefully pour the sauce on top of the leeks. Place the ramekins in a large rectangular oven dish. Add enough hot water to come halfway up the sides of the dishes. Cover the dish tightly with foil. Bake at 180°C (350°F) mark 4 for about 1 hour, or until just firm to the touch. Stand for 4–5 minutes before turning out.

Gratin Dauphinois

POTATOES BAKED IN CREAM

Serve this creamy potato dish with fried or grilled meats.

SERVES 4–6

- 900 G (2 LB) POTATOES, PEELED AND CUT INTO SMALL PIECES
- SALT AND FRESHLY MILLED BLACK PEPPER
- 1 GARLIC CLOVE, CRUSHED
- PINCH OF GRATED NUTMEG
- 150 ML (¼ PINT) SINGLE CREAM
- 75 G (3 OZ) GRUYÈRE CHEESE, GRATED

Cook the potatoes in a saucepan of boiling salted water for 5 minutes, then drain well. Turn into a greased 1.1 litre (2 pint) gratin dish. Stir the seasoning, garlic and nutmeg into the cream and pour over the potatoes. Sprinkle with the cheese.

Cover and bake at 180°C (350°F) mark 4 for about 45 minutes, or until the potatoes are tender. Uncover the dish and brown under a hot grill.

Aubergines à la Nimoise

STUFFED TOMATOES AND AUBERGINES

A traditional recipe from the Languedoc. Ham may be added.

SERVES 8

4 MEDIUM AUBERGINES

SALT AND FRESHLY MILLED BLACK PEPPER

60 ML (4 TBSP) VIRGIN OLIVE OIL

4 LARGE TOMATOES, HALVED

100 G (4 OZ) FRESH WHITE BREADCRUMBS

2 GARLIC CLOVES, CRUSHED

10 ML (2 TSP) CHOPPED FRESH FENNEL

15 ML (1 TBSP) CHOPPED FRESH PARSLEY

15 ML (1 TBSP) CHOPPED FRESH CHIVES

Cut the aubergines in half lengthways, sprinkle the cut sides with salt and set aside for 45 minutes. Dry the cut aubergines well and brush them generously with olive oil on the cut side. Put the aubergines in a large oval gratin dish or rectangular oven dish and cook them under a moderate grill for about 20 minutes, turning once or twice, or until the flesh is very soft. Use a teaspoon to scoop out the flesh, taking care not to break the skins. Chop the flesh finely. Replace the aubergine shells in the dish.

Scoop the pips and pulp out of the tomato halves, using a lemon squeezer or spoon. Reserve the pips and pulp in a bowl. Stand the tomato halves in the dish with the aubergines. Mix the aubergine flesh into the reserved tomato pulp. Add 50 g (2 oz) of the breadcrumbs, the garlic, fennel, parsley, chives and seasoning and mix well.

Use a spoon to divide this stuffing between the aubergine and tomato cases. Sprinkle the remaining breadcrumbs over the stuffed vegetables, then trickle the remaining oil over the top. Bake at 200°C (400°F) mark 6 for 20 minutes, until golden. Serve hot or cold.

Pommes de Terre à la Lyonnaise

SAUTÉ POTATOES WITH ONIONS

Onions are a strong feature of Lyonnais cookery.

SERVES 4–6

675 G (1½ LB) POTATOES, SCRUBBED

SALT AND FRESHLY MILLED BLACK PEPPER

75 G (3 OZ) BUTTER

15 ML (1 TBSP) VEGETABLE OIL

2 ONIONS, SKINNED AND THINLY SLICED

30 ML (2 TBSP) CHOPPED FRESH PARSLEY

Cook the potatoes in their skins in a medium saucepan of boiling salted water for about 20 minutes, or until they are just tender. Drain and leave until cool enough to handle. Peel the potatoes and cut them into 0.5 cm (¼ inch) thick slices.

Heat 50 g (2 oz) of the butter and the oil in a large frying pan. Add the potatoes and cook them until they are crisp and golden brown, turning them several times. Heat the remaining butter in a small frying pan. Add the onions and cook for about 10 minutes until they are golden. Add the onions to the potatoes, stirring them in lightly. Season the mixture to taste and sprinkle with the parsley. Serve at once.

Haricots aux Tomates

BRITTANY-STYLE HARICOT BEANS

Haricots beans are the traditional garnish for the salt meadow (pré-salé) lamb of Brittany. They also make a good accompaniment to a number of other dishes.

SERVES 4

- 225 G (8 OZ) DRIED HARICOT BEANS
- 2 CLOVES
- 2 ONIONS, SKINNED
- 1 BOUQUET GARNI
- 1 GARLIC CLOVE, CRUSHED
- 1 RASHER STREAKY BACON, RINDED AND CHOPPED
- SALT AND FRESHLY MILLED BLACK PEPPER
- 25 G (1 OZ) BUTTER
- 15 ML (1 TBSP) TOMATO PURÉE
- 15 ML (1 TBSP) CHOPPED FRESH PARSLEY

Put the beans in a large saucepan. Cover the beans with plenty of cold water and leave them to soak overnight. Drain the beans and cover with fresh cold water. Stick the cloves in one of the onions, then add it to the pan with the bouquet garni, garlic, bacon and seasoning. Bring to the boil, cover and simmer gently for 1¼–1½ hours or until the beans are tender. Drain, reserving 300 ml (½ pint) of the cooking liquid. Discard the onion and bouquet garni. Rinse out the saucepan.

Finely chop the remaining onion. Melt the butter in the pan. Add the chopped onion and cook it gently for about 5 minutes, then stir in the tomato purée and reserved cooking liquid. Bring to the boil, cover and simmer gently for 10 minutes. Add the drained beans and simmer for a further 10 minutes. Taste and adjust the seasoning, then sprinkle the parsley over the beans and serve.

Petits Pois à la Française

FRENCH-STYLE PEAS WITH LETTUCE

This is a classic method of cooking young fresh peas; however it also transforms frozen peas. For slightly older fresh peas, allow another 5–10 minutes cooking time when blanching the vegetables.

SERVES 6

- 675 G (1½ LB) SHELLED PEAS
- SALT AND FRESHLY MILLED BLACK PEPPER
- 25 G (1 OZ) BUTTER
- 1 BUNCH SPRING ONIONS, TRIMMED AND CHOPPED
- 1 LETTUCE HEART, FINELY SHREDDED
- 150 ML (¼ PINT) CRÈME FRAÎCHE OR SOURED CREAM

If using fresh peas, blanch them first in a medium saucepan of boiling salted water for 5 minutes, then drain. Melt the butter in the saucepan. Add the onions and cook for 2–3 minutes, then stir in the peas and cover the saucepan. Cook for 5 minutes, shaking the pan frequently. Add the lettuce and seasoning and cook gently for a further 5 minutes. Stir in the cream, taste and adjust the seasoning, then serve at once.

Overleaf: Left AUBERGINES NIMOISE *(see page 112), Centre* GRATIN DE POMMES DE TERRE ET COURGETTES *(see page 108), Right* HARICOTS AUX TOMATES *(above)*

Ratatouille

VEGETABLE RAGOUT

Ratatouille is a familiar dish of stewed vegetables, varied in many ways by different cooks. Its origins lie in Nice where it would be prepared using the vegetables below, added at different stages of cooking, stewed in plenty of olive oil until cooked to the taste of the particular cook. Modern versions of this dish simply sauté the vegetables briefly but the true, full-flavour of the complementary vegetables is achieved by longer cooking. Ratatouille is delicious prepared one day, then slowly reheated to boiling point the next day.

SERVES 4–6

- 2 MEDIUM AUBERGINES, TRIMMED AND CUT INTO 2.5 CM (1 INCH) CUBES
- SALT AND FRESHLY MILLED BLACK PEPPER
- 60 ML (4 TBSP) VIRGIN OLIVE OIL
- 2 ONIONS, SKINNED AND SLICED
- 2 GARLIC CLOVES, CRUSHED
- 2 RED OR GREEN PEPPERS, SEEDED AND SLICED
- 1 BOUQUET GARNI
- 4 COURGETTES, TRIMMED AND SLICED
- 4 LARGE TOMATOES, SKINNED AND QUARTERED
- 60 ML (4 TBSP) CHOPPED FRESH PARSLEY

Put the aubergines in a colander. Sprinkle the cubes liberally with salt and place over a bowl for about 20 minutes. This process, known as dégorging, removes bitter juices from the vegetables. Rinse, drain and dry the aubergines well on absorbent kitchen paper. Heat the oil in a large saucepan or casserole. Add the onions and garlic, stir well, then cook for about 10–15 minutes or until the onions are soft but not browned. Add the peppers, aubergines and bouquet garni to the pan and cook them, stirring, for 5 minutes. Stir in the courgettes and seasoning, then cover the saucepan and simmer the vegetables for 15 minutes.

Add the tomatoes, stir lightly and recover the saucepan. Continue cooking the ratatouille for a further 15 minutes, or until all the vegetables are very tender. Taste and adjust the seasoning, discard the bouquet garni, then stir in the parsley and serve. Alternatively, ratatouille may be served cold.

Endives au Fromage Frais

CHICORY WITH FROMAGE FRAIS SAUCE

Choose firm heads of white chicory. A green tinge indicates bitterness and browning is a sign of age.

SERVES 4

- 4 HEADS OF CHICORY, TRIMMED
- 25 G (1 OZ) BUTTER
- 1.25 ML (¼ TSP) GRATED NUTMEG
- 5 ML (1 TSP) LEMON JUICE
- 300 ML (½ PINT) CHICKEN STOCK
- 10 ML (2 TSP) CORNFLOUR
- SALT AND FRESHLY MILLED BLACK PEPPER
- 30 ML (2 TBSP) FROMAGE FRAIS
- CHOPPED FRESH PARSLEY, TO GARNISH

Blanch the chicory in a saucepan of boiling water for 1 minute. Drain, refresh in cold water and drain again. Place the chicory heads in a single layer in a greased gratin dish and dot with the butter. Stir the nutmeg and lemon juice into the stock and pour over the chicory. Cover and cook at 160°C (325°F) mark 3 for 1½ hours, or until the chicory is tender.

Blend the cornflour with 30 ml (2 tbsp) water to a smooth paste. Drain the juice from the dish into a small pan, add the blended cornflour and seasoning. Bring to the boil, stirring, and cook for 1 minute. Add the fromage frais.

Pour the sauce over the chicory and sprinkle with the parsley.

Gratin de Tranches de Pommes de Terre

SCALLOPED POTATOES

Thinly sliced potatoes baked in the oven makes an interesting way of serving this vegetable.

SERVES 4

- 675 G (1½ LB) POTATOES, PEELED AND THINLY SLICED
- SALT AND FRESHLY MILLED BLACK PEPPER
- 45 ML (3 TBSP) PLAIN FLOUR
- 25 G (1 OZ) BUTTER
- 150 ML (¼ PINT) MILK

Arrange the potatoes in layers in a greased gratin dish. Season each layer, dredge with flour and dot with butter. Repeat the layers until all the slices are used, then pour over the milk.

Bake at 190°C (375°F) mark 5 for about 1¼ hours, or until the potatoes are cooked and the top golden brown.

Salade de Feuilles et de Fleurs avec Vinaigrette à l'Huile de Noisette

SALAD LEAVES AND FLOWERS IN HAZELNUT OIL DRESSING

Edible nasturtiums are available in many large supermarkets and specialist greengrocers. In the late summer and early autumn they grow prolifically in the garden and are well worth cultivating for use in salads, and as a garnish or decoration for both sweet and savoury dishes.

SERVES 4

120 ML (8 TBSP) HAZELNUT OIL

30 ML (2 TBSP) LEMON JUICE

5 ML (1 TSP) TARRAGON MUSTARD

SALT AND FRESHLY MILLED BLACK PEPPER

½ OAK LEAF OR BATAVIA LETTUCE, SEPARATED INTO LEAVES

8 RADICCHIO LEAVES

A FEW NASTURTIUM LEAVES

60 ML (4 TBSP) FINELY CHOPPED MIXED FRESH HERBS (INCLUDING TARRAGON)

60 ML (4 TBSP) COARSELY CHOPPED HAZELNUTS

A FEW NASTURTIUM FLOWERS

To make the dressing, put the oil and lemon juice in a large bowl with the mustard and seasoning to taste. Whisk with a fork until thickened.

Tear the lettuce, radicchio and nasturtium leaves into the bowl. Add the herbs and toss gently until the leaves are coated in the dressing.

To serve, transfer the salad to a serving bowl and sprinkle over the hazelnuts. Arrange the nasturtium flowers amongst the salad leaves.

Haricots Verts à la Crème

GREEN BEANS IN A CREAM SAUCE

These slender, stringless beans, with a delicate flavour, are best steamed.

SERVES 4

450 G (1 LB) GREEN BEANS, TOPPED AND TAILED

25 G (1 OZ) BUTTER

15 ML (1 TBSP) DOUBLE CREAM

1 EGG YOLK

FRESHLY MILLED BLACK PEPPER

15 ML (1 TBSP) CHOPPED FRESH PARSLEY

Cook the beans in a steamer over a cocotte for about 15 minutes until 'al dente'. Drain and transfer to a serving dish, keep hot. Heat the butter and cream together in a saucepan, remove from heat and gradually whisk in the egg yolk. Return to the heat and cook gently without boiling. Add seasoning and parsley, then pour over the beans.

ASPERGES À LA SAUCE MOUSSELINE *(see page 110)*

Chicorée Frisée au Orange et aux Croûtons

CURLY ENDIVE WITH ORANGE AND CROÛTONS

Although native to the Mediterranean, curly endive is now grown in the temperate countries throughout the world, and is available virtually all year round. At its best, curly endive is crisp, pale green and frondy, with a mildly bitter flavour. It does not keep well and quickly goes limp and yellow. Most heads of endive are very large, but some greengrocers will split them in halves or quarters. Take care not to confuse curly endive with the torpedo-shaped chicory. In France, chicory is called endive, whereas curly endive is called chicorée frisée.

SERVES 8

2 THICK SLICES OF WHITE BREAD

VEGETABLE OIL, FOR SHALLOW FRYING

SALT AND FRESHLY MILLED BLACK PEPPER

1 LARGE HEAD OF CURLY ENDIVE

½ BUNCH OF WATERCRESS

2 LARGE ORANGES

60 ML (4 TBSP) OLIVE OIL

60 ML (4 TBSP) WHITE WINE VINEGAR

2.5 ML (½ TSP) CASTER SUGAR

Cut the crusts off the bread and cut the bread into 1 cm (½ inch) cubes. Heat the vegetable oil in a frying pan. Add the cubes of bread and fry until crisp and golden. Remove the croûtons with a slotted spoon and drain well on absorbent kitchen paper. Sprinkle with salt and cool.

Remove and discard any coarse or discoloured leaves from the endive. Tear the endive into pieces, wash and dry thoroughly. Wash, trim and dry the watercress.

With a small serrated knife and working over a bowl to catch the juices, cut away all the skin and pith from the oranges. Reserve the juices. Cut the orange flesh into segments, leaving the membrane behind. Remove any pips with the tip of the knife. Arrange the endive, watercress and orange in a serving bowl.

Whisk the reserved orange juice with the olive oil, vinegar, sugar and seasoning to taste in a jug. Pour over the salad and add the croûtons just before serving.

Salade de Printemps

SPRING SALAD

Select the freshest salad vegetables and wash and dry them well.

SERVES 6

2 HEADS OF CHICORY, SLICED

225 G (8 OZ) LAMB'S LETTUCE

225 G (8 OZ) YOUNG DANDELION LEAVES

1 SMALL RADICCHIO

225 G (8 OZ) FIRM MUSHROOMS, THINLY SLICED

2 SHALLOTS, SKINNED AND FINELY CHOPPED

10 ML (2 TSP) CHOPPED FRESH PARSLEY

30 ML (2 TBSP) SAUCE VINAIGRETTE (SEE PAGE 128)

Mix all the salad ingredients together, shredding those leaves that are large. Just before serving, toss the salad in the vinaigrette dressing.

SAUCES, DRESSINGS AND MARINADES

Beurre Blanc

WHITE BUTTER SAUCE

Traditionally served in the regions of Nantes and Anjou with poached, Loire-caught pike or shad, this sauce is also superb with trout and salmon steaks. Make this buttery sauce when you are ready to serve it as it does not tolerate being kept waiting.

SERVES 4–6

- 3–4 SHALLOTS, SKINNED AND FINELY CHOPPED
- 45 ML (3 TBSP) WHITE WINE VINEGAR
- 45 ML (3 TBSP) DRY WHITE WINE
- 175 G (6 OZ) UNSALTED BUTTER, CUT INTO CUBES
- SALT AND FRESHLY MILLED BLACK PEPPER

Put the shallots in a small saucepan with the vinegar and wine. Put over a medium heat and bring to the boil, then continue to boil, uncovered until the liquid is reduced by about one third. There should be about 30 ml (2 tbsp) of liquid left – you will have to use judgement in assessing the quantity but look for a thin covering in the base of the pan. Turn the heat to the lowest possible setting under the saucepan and begin to whisk the reduced liquor. Add a piece of butter and whisk continuously until softened and creamy before adding another piece of butter. Continue in this way, slowly adding the butter, and the sauce will become quite creamy. When all the butter is added the sauce should be creamy; do not continue to cook. Season the sauce, pour it into a heated sauceboat and serve at once. If you do have to keep the sauce warm, stand the sauceboat in a dish of hot water until you are ready to serve the *beurre blanc*. On no account allow any drops of water to enter the sauce.

Sauce Bercy

BERCY SAUCE

This classic sauce takes its name from a region of Paris, Bercy, which was once home of the most prominent wine-market in Europe and known for the fine cellars in the region. Often dishes which include wine sauce take the title 'Bercy'; however the sauce is traditionally served with fish. It is also good with vegetables or light meals and poultry for which suitable stocks should be substituted.

SERVES 4–6

- 65 G (2½ OZ) BUTTER
- 50 G (2 OZ) SHALLOTS, SKINNED AND FINELY CHOPPED
- 150 ML (¼ PINT) DRY WHITE WINE
- 300 ML (½ PINT) GOOD FISH STOCK
- 15 G (½ OZ) PLAIN FLOUR
- JUICE OF ½ LEMON
- SALT AND FRESHLY MILLED BLACK PEPPER
- 30 ML (2 TBSP) CHOPPED FRESH PARSLEY

Melt 15 g (½ oz) of the butter in a small saucepan. Add the shallots and cook them gently until they are soft but not browned. Pour in the wine and half the stock. Bring to the boil, then boil, uncovered, until the liquid is reduced by half.

Meanwhile, soften half the remaining butter, then beat in the flour to make a smooth paste, or beurre manié. Pour the remaining stock into the saucepan and bring the sauce to the boil. Whisking all the time, add the beurre manié bit by bit and continue whisking until the sauce boils and thickens. Add the lemon juice, simmer the sauce gently for 2 minutes, then take the saucepan off the heat. Whisk in seasoning to taste, the parsley and the remaining butter, then pour the sauce into a heated sauceboat and serve.

Sauce de Tomates

TOMATO SAUCE

It is important for this sauce to choose tomatoes which have a really good flavour or the end result will be insipid.

SERVES 4–6

- 30 ML (2 TBSP) OLIVE OIL
- 2 GARLIC CLOVES, CRUSHED
- 1 ONION, SKINNED AND FINELY CHOPPED
- 1 RASHER STREAKY BACON, RINDED AND CHOPPED
- 675 G (1½ LB) RIPE TOMATOES, SKINNED AND CHOPPED
- SALT AND FRESHLY MILLED BLACK PEPPER
- 5 ML (1 TSP) SUGAR
- 15 ML (1 TBSP) STRAWBERRY OR RASPBERRY VINEGAR
- 15 ML (1 TBSP) CHOPPED FRESH BASIL
- SALT AND FRESHLY MILLED BLACK PEPPER

Heat the oil in a medium saucepan. Add the garlic, onion and bacon, and cook gently for 5 minutes, stirring occasionally. Stir in the tomatoes, seasoning, sugar, fruit vinegar and basil. Cover the saucepan and simmer the ingredients gently for 30 minutes, or until the tomatoes are pulpy.

Pureé the sauce in a blender or food processor, then sieve it to remove all the tomato pips and pieces of skin. Reheat the sauce, taste and adjust the seasoning before serving either hot or cold.

Sauce Hollandaise

HOLLANDAISE SAUCE

Hollandaise sauce is served warm with fish or vegetables. It may be kept warm by placing the sauceboat in a dish of hot water but for no longer than 15-20 minutes.

SERVES 4: MAKES ABOUT 150 ML (¼ PINT)

- JUICE OF ½ LEMON
- 5 ML (1 TSP) WATER
- SALT AND FRESHLY MILLED BLACK OR WHITE PEPPER
- 2 EGG YOLKS
- 100 G (4 OZ) UNSALTED BUTTER, SOFTENED

Half fill a small saucepan with water. Bring to the boil, then lower the heat until the water is just simmering. Put the lemon juice, water and seasoning into a basin that will fit neatly into the top of the pan. Add the egg yolks and a small piece of the butter and beat well with a whisk or wooden spoon until the mixture is thick. Add the remaining butter to the egg yolks, a dessertspoonful at a time, whisking well.

When all the butter has been incorporated, the sauce should be thick and glossy. Taste and adjust the seasoning, then transfer it to a heated sauceboat and serve.

Sauce Béarnaise

BÉARNAISE SAUCE

Created by a chef circa 1830 at the Pavillon Henri IV at Saint Germain, béarnaise sauce is flavoured with tarragon and chervil to serve with grilled meats and steaks. In this recipe the butter is added in small knobs rather than being melted and cooled: both methods are acceptable and interchangeable.

SERVES 4: MAKES A SCANT 150 ML (¼ PINT)

60 ML (4 TBSP) WHITE WINE VINEGAR

6 BLACK OR WHITE PEPPERCORNS

1 TARRAGON SPRIG

1 CHERVIL SPRIG

1 SMALL SHALLOT, SKINNED AND FINELY CHOPPED

2 PERFECTLY FRESH EGG YOLKS

75 G (3 OZ) UNSALTED BUTTER, SOFTENED

2.5 ML (½ TSP) CHOPPED FRESH TARRAGON

2.5 ML (½ TSP) CHOPPED FRESH CHERVIL

SALT AND FRESHLY MILLED WHITE PEPPER

Put the vinegar, peppercorns, tarragon and chervil sprigs, and the shallot in a small saucepan. Bring to the boil, then boil until the liquid is reduced to a scant 15 ml (1 tbsp). Strain the liquid into a basin and add the egg yolks. Whisk well until the eggs are pale and frothy, then whisk in a small knob of butter. Rinse out the saucepan and half fill it with water. Bring this to the boil, then reduce the heat so that the water is barely simmering. Put the basin over the water and add the butter in small knobs, whisking all the time. Add more butter only when the previous knob is thoroughly mixed in. When all the butter has been incorporated, stir in the chopped tarragon and chervil and add seasoning to taste. The sauce should be thick and glossy. Serve at once.

Aïoli

GARLIC MAYONNAISE

Often described as 'the butter of Provence', aioli is traditionally served with cold poached cod and potatoes, but it makes an excellent accompaniment to almost any cold meat, fish or vegetables.

MAKES 300 ML (½ PINT)

3–4 GARLIC CLOVES, CRUSHED

2 PERFECTLY FRESH EGG YOLKS

SALT AND FRESHLY MILLED BLACK PEPPER

300 ML (½ PINT) OLIVE OIL

Follow the method for making Mayonnaise (see page 125), adding the garlic to the egg yolks. This sauce does not use any vinegar.

Sauce Rémoulade

RÉMOULADE SAUCE

A sauce that is traditionally served with cold meat, poultry or shellfish, and also grilled meats and fish. It is also one of the sauces for Fondue bourguignonne (see page 98).

MAKES A GENEROUS 300 ML (½ PINT)

300 ML (½ PINT) MAYONNAISE (SEE PAGE 125)

10 ML (2 TSP) FRENCH MUSTARD

10 ML (2 TSP) CHOPPED CAPERS

15 ML (1 TBSP) CHOPPED FRESH PARSLEY

5 ML (1 TSP) CHOPPED FRESH TARRAGON

5 ML (1 TSP) CHOPPED FRESH CHERVIL

Mix the mayonnaise into a bowl with all the flavouring ingredients. Cover and set aside for at least 30 minutes before serving so that the flavours have time to infuse.

Mayonnaise

MAYONNAISE

Using olive oil to make mayonnaise gives the sauce a distinctive, flavour; if you prefer, you can substitute a part-quantity oil of your choice for the olive oil.

MAKES A GENEROUS 300 ML (½ PINT)

2 PERFECTLY FRESH EGG YOLKS

2.5 ML (½ TSP) SALT

5 ML (1 TSP) FRENCH MUSTARD

FRESHLY MILLED BLACK PEPPER

30 ML (2 TBSP) WINE VINEGAR

300 ML (½ PINT) OLIVE OIL

To obtain the best results, all the ingredients should be at room temperature. You can make mayonnaise with eggs straight from the refrigerator but there is a greater chance of it curdling.

Put the egg yolks, salt, mustard, pepper and 15ml (1 tbsp) of the vinegar into a blender or food processor. Blend together until thoroughly combined. With the motor running, gradually trickle in the oil, drop by drop at first, then in a thin steady stream until it has all been incorporated. Finally, add the remaining vinegar.

Alternatively, whisk the egg yolks with the other ingredients in a large basin, then whisk in the oil, drop by drop.

When about half the oil is incorporated, and the mixture is thick and shiny, the remaining oil may be added in a steady trickle. Taste and adjust the seasoning before serving.

Sauce Tartare

TARTARE SAUCE

Tartare sauce is the classic accompaniment to fried fish.

MAKES A GENEROUS 300 ML (½ PINT)

300 ML (½ PINT) MAYONNAISE

30 ML (2 TBSP) FINELY CHOPPED GHERKINS

15 ML (1 TBSP) CHOPPED FRESH PARSLEY

15 ML (1 TBSP) CHOPPED CAPERS

Mix the mayonnaise with all the flavouring ingredients. Cover and leave the sauce for at least 30 minutes before serving so that the flavours have time to infuse.

Sauce Gribiche

HERB AND CAPER SAUCE

An excellent alternative to rémoulade sauce, this sauce is made from cooked, rather than raw, eggs. The method of combining ingredients is the same as for Mayonnaise (see page 125), using a blender or food processor (as below) or the sauce may be prepared by hand following the recipe for mayonnaise.

MAKES A SCANT 450 ML (¾ PINT)

2 EGGS

SALT AND FRESHLY MILLED BLACK PEPPER

5 ML (1 TSP) FRENCH MUSTARD

300 ML (½ PINT) OLIVE OIL

15 ML (1 TBSP) WINE VINEGAR

4 GHERKINS, FINELY CHOPPED

15 ML (1 TBSP) CHOPPED FRESH PARSLEY

5 ML (1 TSP) CHOPPED FRESH TARRAGON

10 ML (2 TSP) CHOPPED CAPERS

Cook the eggs in a small saucepan of boiling water for 10 minutes. Cool them under cold water and remove their shells. Cut the eggs in half, take out the yolks and put them in a blender or food processor. Add the salt, pepper and mustard to the yolks.

With the machine running, add the oil drop by drop at first, then in a fine even trickle. When half the oil has been incorporated, add the vinegar, then slowly trickle in the remaining oil. Transfer the sauce to a basin and stir in the gherkins, parsley, tarragon and capers. Finely chop the egg whites, then stir them into the sauce. Taste and adjust the seasoning.

Sauce au Cassis

BLACKCURRANT LIQUEUR DRESSING

This will appeal to anyone who likes a slightly sweet dressing. It is excellent with a simple green salad to which some freshly chopped mint or basil has been added. Other fruit liqueurs may be used in place of cassis, for example framboise (raspberry) or fraises des bois (strawberry) if preferred.

MAKES 75 ML (5 TBSP)

45 ML (3 TBSP) OLIVE OIL

15 ML (1 TBSP) RED WINE VINEGAR

15 ML (1 TBSP) CRÈME DE CASSIS

SALT AND FRESHLY MILLED BLACK PEPPER

Put all the ingredients in a screw-topped jar and shake well until they are emulsified. Use at once.

Sauce Ravigote

RAVIGOTE SAUCE

There are two classic versions of this sauce: this is the cold one, based on a vinaigrette dressing; the alternative is a hot sauce, thickened with flour, then sharpened with vinegar.

MAKES A SCANT 300 ML (½ PINT)

½ BUNCH WATERCRESS

30 ML (2 TBSP) RED WINE VINEGAR

2.5 ML (½ TSP) FRENCH WHOLEGRAIN MUSTARD

150 ML (¼ PINT) VIRGIN OLIVE OIL

SALT AND FRESHLY MILLED BLACK PEPPER

15 ML (1 TBSP) CHOPPED FRESH PARSLEY

15 ML (1 TBSP) CHOPPED FRESH CHIVES

15 ML (1 TBSP) CHOPPED FRESH TARRAGON

15 ML (1 TBSP) CHOPPED FRESH CHERVIL

15 ML (1 TBSP) FINELY CHOPPED ONION

Chop off 2.5 cm (1 inch) of the watercress stalks. Purée all the ingredients, with the exception of the salt, in a blender or food processor until smooth. Taste and add a little salt, if necessary.

Pistou

PISTOU

Pistou is very similar to Italian pesto. *Both sauces are based on fresh basil, garlic and olive oil with cheese added. The Italian version also has pine nuts pounded into it.*

50 G (2 OZ) FRESH BASIL LEAVES

2 GARLIC CLOVES

PINCH OF SALT

50 G (2 OZ) FRESHLY GRATED PARMESAN CHEESE

60 ML (4 TBSP) VIRGIN OLIVE OIL

Remove any stalks from the basil and pound the leaves in a mortar with the garlic and salt. When smooth and the leaves are reduced to a green paste, pound in the cheese. Gradually add the olive oil, stirring steadily so that it is thoroughly combined with the paste. Alternatively, purée the basil, garlic and salt in a blender or food processor. Add the cheese and slowly pour in the oil with the machine running.

SAUCE VINAIGRETTE

VINAIGRETTE DRESSING

Undoubtedly the most useful basic dressing and one that may be varied in many different ways. The proportion of oil to vinegar is open to discussion as individual preferences vary. One part vinegar to three parts oil is a fairly standard amount, although this can be made more acidic by using more vinegar and less oil. The oil may be varied in type according to the salad that is being dressed: olive oil, virgin olive oil, hazelnut oil, walnut oil and corn oil are the ones most frequently used in French cookery. As a general rule red wine vinegars are used for basic green salads and meats; white wine vinegars are used with white meats and some vegetables; tarragon vinegar is used with fish and white meats; and lemon juice is used with fish, some vegetables and salads. It is important to remember that any dressing is intended to complement the salad, not dominate it.

MAKES 60 ML (4 TBSP)

45 ML (3 TBSP) OIL

15 ML (1 TBSP) VINEGAR OR LEMON JUICE

1.25 ML (¼ TSP) FRENCH MUSTARD

SALT AND FRESHLY MILLED BLACK PEPPER

Put all the ingredients into a screw-topped jar, shake well and use as required.

ROUILLE

PIMENTO AND GARLIC SAUCE

This piquant, garlicky sauce is an essential accompaniment to Bouillabaisse (see page 20).

MAKES ABOUT 300 ML (½ PINT)

25 G (1 OZ) PIMENTO, CHOPPED

1 MEDIUM POTATO, PEELED AND BOILED

4 GARLIC CLOVES, CRUSHED

15 ML (1 TBSP) BASIL OR THYME

TABASCO SAUCE, TO TASTE

150 ML (¼ PINT) OLIVE OIL

SALT AND FRESHLY MILLED BLACK PEPPER

Pound the first five ingredients in a bowl to form a smooth paste. Gradually add the oil, beating the mixture all the time as for mayonnaise. Season to taste. Alternatively, blend the first five ingredients into a paste in a food processor. Gradually add the oil while the machine is running to form a mayonnaise-like texture. Season to taste.

Huile Provençale

SPICY HERB OIL

This oil is used extensively to brush over meat before grilling and for barbecues. A few tablespoons added to the oil for a Fondue bourguinonne (page 98) will give the meat added flavour.

MAKES 600 ML (1 PINT)

- 2 ROSEMARY SPRIGS
- 2 BAY LEAVES
- 6 THYME SPRIGS
- 1 LARGE GARLIC CLOVE, SKINNED
- 4 RED CHILLIES
- 10 BLACK PEPPERCORNS
- 6 JUNIPER BERRIES
- 20 CORIANDER SEEDS
- 600 ML (1 PINT) VIRGIN OLIVE OIL

Wash the herbs and dry them thoroughly. Pack the herbs into a glass bottle with a stopper. Add the garlic, chillies, peppercorns, juniper berries and coriander seeds. Pour the oil into the bottle, close it tightly and leave for at least 2–3 weeks before using.

Marinade de Vin Rouge

RED WINE MARINADE

This marinade is suitable for both beef and lamb. Not only will it flavour the meat, it also helps to tenderise it before cooking. Most meats benefit from being left in a red wine marinade for 1–2 days. This quantity of marinade may be used for up to 1.8 kg (4 lb) of meat.

MAKES 600 ML (1 PINT)

- 2 CARROTS, PEELED AND SLICED
- 2 GARLIC CLOVES, CRUSHED
- 1 MEDIUM ONION, SKINNED AND CHOPPED
- 1 BAY LEAF
- 3 PARSLEY SPRIGS
- 1 ROSEMARY SPRIG
- 1 THYME SPRIG
- 1 MARJORAM SPRIG
- 2–3 CLOVES
- ABOUT 6 BLACK PEPPERCORNS
- 2.5 ML (½ TSP) SALT
- 600 ML (1 PINT) FULL-BODIED RED WINE

Put all the ingredients in a medium saucepan and heat them slowly to just below boiling point. Remove from the heat and allow to cool, then pour the marinade over the meat. Cover and leave in the refrigerator, turning the meat occasionally.

Marinade de Citron

LEMON MARINADE

This marinade may be used for chicken or veal but is most suitable for fish. Fish that has been marinated for as little as 30 minutes prior to grilling, remains moist and full of flavour. This quantity of marinade is sufficient for 6 fillets of flat fish (sole or plaice) or 900 g (2 lb) large fillets (cod or haddock) or cutlets.

---

60 ML (4 TBSP) OLIVE OIL

JUICE OF 1 LARGE LEMON

2.5 ML (½ TSP) SALT

6 BLACK PEPPERCORNS

10 CORIANDER SEEDS, CRUSHED

1 GARLIC CLOVE, SKINNED AND SLICED (OPTIONAL)

15 ML (1 TBSP) CHOPPED FRESH FENNEL *OR* 10 ML (2 TSP) CHOPPED FRESH TARRAGON

Mix all the marinade ingredients together in a basin and whisk well. Place fish in a gratin dish. Pour the marinade over and cover. Leave for 30 minutes to 4 hours turning two or three times.

Marinade de Vin Blanc

WHITE WINE MARINADE

This marinade is suitable for chicken, guinea fowl, turkey, veal, pork or lamb. It is sufficient for approximately 6 chicken joints or pork chops, or a 1.4 kg (3 lb) joint of meat.

---

150 ML (¼ PINT) DRY WHITE WINE

60 ML (4 TBSP) OLIVE OIL

2.5 ML (½ TSP) SALT

12 BLACK PEPPERCORNS

1 BAY LEAF

1 GARLIC CLOVE, SKINNED AND SLICED

1 SHALLOT, SKINNED AND FINELY CHOPPED

1 ROSEMARY OR MARJORAM SPRIG

Combine all the ingredients in a jug or bowl and whisk until well mixed. Pour the marinade over the ingredients, cover and leave in the refrigerator for a few hours, or up to 2 days, turning from time to time.

DESSERTS

Clafoutis aux Cerises de Limousin

BAKED CHERRY PUDDING

Clafoutis of various kinds are made throughout France, but the cherry one from Limousin is the best known. Other fruit may be used, such as plums, apples or grapes.

SERVES 6

15 G (½ OZ) BUTTER PLUS EXTRA FOR GREASING

675 G (1½ LB) CHERRIES, STONED

75 G (3 OZ) CASTER SUGAR

15 ML (1 TBSP) BRANDY (OPTIONAL)

225 G (8 OZ) PLAIN FLOUR

PINCH OF SALT

3 EGGS, SEPARATED

350 ML (12 FL OZ) MILK

Thoroughly butter a large oval gratin dish. Put the cherries in the dish. Sprinkle with 25 g (1 oz) of the sugar and the brandy if using.

Sift the flour and salt into a bowl. Stir in the remaining sugar. Make a well in the dry ingredients, add the egg yolks and a little milk. Beat the yolks and milk, gradually working in the flour and adding the remaining milk to make a smooth pouring batter. Whisk the egg whites until they form soft peaks, then fold them into the batter. Pour the batter over the cherries and dot with the butter.

Bake the clafoutis at 190°C (375°F) mark 5 for about 40 minutes, or until the batter is well risen, set and golden brown. Serve warm with cream.

Soufflé aux Pruneaux

PRUNE SOUFFLÉ

Served with fresh cream, this delectable soufflé makes a perfect ending to a meal.

SERVES 8-10

450 G (1 LB) PRUNES

450 ML (¾ PINT) DRY WHITE WINE

GRATED RIND AND JUICE OF 2 ORANGES

75 G (3 OZ) SUGAR

8 EGG WHITES

Put the prunes in a medium saucepan. Pour in the wine and add the orange rind and juice. Leave the prunes to soak in this liquid overnight. Stir in the sugar, cover and simmer gently for about 1 hour or until they are tender. Strain the prunes, reserving the juice. Stone, then purée them with the reserved juice in a blender or food processor. Thoroughly butter a 2.5 litre (4¼ pint) soufflé dish. Whisk the egg whites until they form soft peaks, then fold them into the prune purée. Turn the mixture into the soufflé dish and bake at 160°C (325°F) mark 3 for 1 hour, or until the soufflé is well risen. Remove from the oven and serve at once.

Note: If it is cooked in a fan-assisted oven the soufflé will be ready in about 45 minutes.

Poires Agenaises

PEARS WITH PRUNES

A good combination for a winter dessert.

SERVES 4–6

225 G (8 OZ) PRUNES, PREFERABLY FROM AGEN

300 ML (½ PINT) DRY RED OR WHITE WINE

JUICE OF ½ LEMON

100 G (4 OZ) SUGAR

1 VANILLA POD

450 G (1 LB) SMALL FIRM PEARS

Place the prunes in a large saucepan. Pour the wine over them, then cover the pan and leave the fruit to soak overnight or for several hours.

Add the lemon juice, sugar and vanilla pod to the prunes and wine. Bring them slowly to the boil over low heat. Meanwhile, peel, core and quarter the pears and add them to the pan just before the liquid boils. Lower the heat, cover the pan and simmer the fruit gently for about 30 minutes or until the prunes and pears are quite tender.

Taste the liquor and add extra sugar, if necessary, then remove the vanilla pod. Serve the fruit warm or allow it to cool before serving with cream.

Pêches Flambées

PEACHES IN BRANDY

Choose peaches that are just ripe for this dish.

SERVES 4

300 ML (½ PINT) WATER

100 G (4 OZ) SUGAR

1 VANILLA POD

4 LARGE PEACHES

60 ML (4 TBSP) BRANDY

Put the water, sugar and vanilla pod in a medium saucepan. Heat gently until the sugar has dissolved, then simmer for 5 minutes.

Plunge the peaches into boiling water for 1 minute, drain and rinse under cold water, then peel off their skins. Cut the peaches in half and remove their stones.

Add the peaches to the sugar syrup and poach them gently for about 4 minutes or until just tender. Use a draining spoon to remove the peaches from the pan. Put the fruit in a large round gratin dish and keep them warm.

Remove the vanilla pod, then boil the sugar syrup rapidly until it is reduced by about half. Pour the reduced syrup over the peaches.

Pour the brandy into the saucepan and heat it very gently for a few seconds. Pour the warm brandy over the peaches and ignite them.

Serve with cream.

Crêpes aux Pommes
APPLE PANCAKES

These pancakes are a speciality of the Périgord.

SERVES 4–6

1 QUANTITY CRÊPE BATTER (SEE PAGE 156)
2 MEDIUM EATING APPLES, PEELED, CORED AND VERY THINLY SLICED
30 ML (2 TBSP) LEMON JUICE
50 G (2 OZ) CASTER SUGAR
OIL FOR FRYING

Make the batter following the recipe instructions. Place the apples in a gratin dish and sprinkle with the lemon juice and half the sugar.

Heat a very little oil in a 24 cm (9½ inch) crêpe pan. Pour in a little of the batter, tilting the pan to spread it quickly and evenly. Scatter a sixth of the apple slices over the batter and cook for about 30 seconds, then pour a little more of the batter over the apples. Cook until the underside of the pancake is golden brown, then turn it over and cook the second side until it is golden.

Slide the pancake out of the crêpe pan on to a serving plate, sprinkle with some of the remaining sugar and serve at once. Cook the remaining batter and apples in the same way.

Crêpes au Grand Marnier
GRAND MARNIER CRÊPES

Nothing is more welcome after a day's skiing than a hot crêpe, well-laced with Grand Marnier. 'Crêpe kiosks' selling these thin pancakes straight out of the pan, abound in most French ski resorts.

SERVES 6

1 QUANTITY CRÊPE BATTER (SEE PAGE 156)
90 ML (6 TBSP) GRAND MARNIER
ABOUT 30 ML (2 TBSP) CASTER SUGAR

Make the crêpes following the recipe instructions. Slide each one out of the pan and sprinkle with a tablespoon of the Grand Marnier and a little sugar. Roll up and serve at once.

CRÊPES AU GRAND MARNIER

Gâteau de Marrons

CHESTNUT MOULD

SERVES 4

450 G (1 LB) CHESTNUTS

150 ML (¼ PINT) MILK

100 G (4 OZ) SUGAR

GRATED RIND AND JUICE OF 1 SMALL ORANGE

BUTTER FOR GREASING

15 ML (1 TBSP) RUM OR BRANDY, OPTIONAL

2 EGG WHITES

TO DECORATE: WHIPPED CREAM, MARRONS GLACÉ (OPTIONAL)

Peel the chestnuts removing all traces of the brown skin (see page 72). Put the chestnuts in a medium saucepan with the milk, half the sugar and the orange rind. Heat until simmering, then cook gently for 20 minutes or until the chestnuts are very soft.

Lightly butter a 15 cm (6 inch) cake tin. Place the remaining sugar in a small saucepan. Stir in 45 ml (3 tbsp) water and heat gently until the sugar has dissolved, then boil rapidly until the syrup turns to a pale golden brown. Remove the pan from the heat and immediately pour the caramel into the base of the prepared tin. Leave to cool.

Purée the chestnuts with half the milk in a blender or food processor. Add the orange juice and rum or brandy, if using. Whisk the egg whites until they form soft peaks, then fold them into the chestnut purée. Pour hot water to a depth of 2.5 cm (1 inch) into a large round gratin dish. Spoon the mixture into the cake tin and stand it in the gratin dish. Bake the chestnut mould at 160°C (325°F) mark 3 for 35–40 minutes or until set. Leave to cool, then chill for several hours or overnight.

Turn the mould out of the tin on to a plate just before serving. Decorate.

Macarons au Chocolat

MACAROONS WITH CHOCOLATE

A rich dessert which makes a perfect ending to any meal.

SERVES 6–8

12 ALMOND MACAROONS

60 ML (4 TBSP) RUM

100 G (4 OZ) BUTTER

100 G (4 OZ) CASTER SUGAR

150 ML (¼ PINT) MILK

1 EGG

225 G (8 OZ) PLAIN CHOCOLATE, BROKEN INTO SMALL PIECES

Place the macaroons on a flat dish and sprinkle with the rum. Cream the butter and sugar together until light and fluffy. Pour the milk into a small saucepan and bring it just to the boil. Remove the saucepan from the heat and leave the milk to cool for 10 minutes, then beat in the egg.

Half fill a small saucepan with water and heat it until it is almost simmering. Put the chocolate in a basin and stand it over the pan of water. Turn the heat to low so that the water does not boil. When the chocolate has melted, slowly stir in the milk, still on the heat. Add the butter and sugar. Whisk the sauce until it is very smooth.

Place four of the macaroons in the base of a serving dish. Pour half the chocolate sauce over them, then top it with four more macaroons. Pour in the remaining chocolate sauce and finally add the last of the macaroons. Cool, then place the dish in the refrigerator for at least 12 hours.

Oranges au Caramel

ORANGES IN CARAMEL

A heavy saucepan is essential for making this caramel.

SERVES 6

225 G (8 OZ) GRANULATED SUGAR
300 ML (½ PINT) WATER
6 MEDIUM ORANGES

Put half the sugar into a heavy saucepan. Heat gently until the sugar melts then caramelises (this may take some time and should not be hurried). Do not stir but tilt the pan to even out the colour of the sugar. When the caramel is a deep golden brown, remove the pan from the heat and gradually add the water. It may splutter so protect your hands. Add the remaining sugar, stir until smooth and bring to the boil. Boil until it is a thick syrup. Cool thoroughly.

Peel the oranges, removing all the white pith and pips. Cut the oranges into thick slices. Put into a glass dish and spoon over the caramel. Chill well before serving.

Sorbet aux Raisins

GRAPE SORBET

Flavoured with kirsch, this refreshing sorbet is easy to prepare. The grapes require no peeling or seeding as the mixture is sieved to remove them.

SERVES 6

900 G (2 LB) BLACK GRAPES
100 G (4 OZ) GRANULATED SUGAR
10 ML (2 TSP) LEMON JUICE
1 EGG WHITE
45 ML (3 TBSP) KIRSCH
LANGUES DE CHATS, TO SERVE

Remove the grapes off the stalks but do not bother to peel or seed them.

Put the sugar in a heavy-based saucepan with 450 ml (¾ pint) water and heat gently until the sugar has dissolved. Bring to the boil and bubble for 5 minutes. Remove from the heat, stir in the lemon juice, then cool slightly.

Put the grapes and sugar syrup together in a blender or food processor and work to a purée. Sieve to remove the seeds and skin. Pour into a shallow freezer container and freeze for 4–5 hours or until the mixture is beginning to set. Remove the sorbet from the freezer and mash with a fork to break down the ice crystals.

Whisk the egg white lightly, then fold the kirsch and egg white into the sorbet. Return to the freezer and freeze for at least a further 2 hours, or until firm. Serve the grape sorbet straight from the freezer, with langues de chats handed separately.

Tarte au Citron

LEMON TART

SERVES 8

1 QUANTITY PÂTE BRISÉE (SEE PAGE 156)

175 G (6 OZ) CASTER SUGAR

100 G (4 OZ) UNSALTED BUTTER

3 EGGS

3 LEMONS

Make the pastry following the recipe instructions, adding 50 g (2 oz) caster sugar to the dry ingredients. Roll out the pastry and use it to line a 26 cm (10¼ inch) flan dish. Prick the base lightly. Place a sheet of greaseproof paper in the pastry case and top with dried peas or baking beans. Bake at 200°C (400°F) mark 6 for 10 minutes. Remove the paper and beans and bake the pastry case for a further 5 minutes to dry out the base. Melt the butter and cool it slightly. Whisk the eggs. Grate the rinds from all the lemons and add it to the eggs. Take off five thin slices from one lemon and reserve these for decoration. Squeeze the juice from the remaining lemons, then add it to the eggs. Whisk in the remaining sugar, then whisk in the butter.

Pour the lemon mixture into the pastry case and bake the tart at 160°C (325°F) mark 3 for 12–15 minutes, until the filling is just set. While the filling is cooking remove all the pith and any pips from the reserved lemon slices. Lay these in a circle on top of the filling and return the tart to the oven for a further 5 minutes. Allow to cool, then chill lightly.

TARTE AU CITRON

Tarte Tropezienne

CRÈME PÂTISSIÈRE-FILLED TART

This very simple tart consists of a rich yeasted dough filled with crème pâtissière.

SERVES 8

100 ML (4 FL OZ) MILK
25 G (1 OZ) CASTER SUGAR
10 ML (2 TSP) DRIED YEAST
250 G (10 OZ) STRONG PLAIN FLOUR
2.5 ML (½ TSP) SALT
75 G (3 OZ) UNSALTED BUTTER
3 EGGS, LIGHTLY BEATEN

CRÈME PÂTISSIÈRE:
4 EGGS
75 G (3 OZ) VANILLA SUGAR
50 G (2 OZ) PLAIN FLOUR
600 ML (1 PINT) MILK
5 ML (1 TSP) VANILLA ESSENCE
50 G (2 OZ) UNSALTED BUTTER
45 ML (3 TBSP) DOUBLE CREAM
ICING SUGAR TO DUST

Thoroughly butter a 26 cm (10¼ inch) flan dish and dust it evenly with flour. Line the base with a circle of greaseproof paper. Heat the milk until lukewarm. Stir in 5 ml (1 tsp) of the sugar and sprinkle the dried yeast over the milk. Set aside in a warm place for about 10 minutes or until the yeast liquid is frothy. Sift the flour and salt into a bowl, then rub in the butter. Add the remaining sugar, then mix in the yeast liquid and eggs to make a thick batter. Beat until smooth.

Spread the batter into the prepared flan case, cover with a piece of oiled cling film and leave in a warm place until the batter has doubled in size – about 2 hours. Discard the cling film. Bake at 220°C (425°F) mark 7 for 10 minutes. Cover with a piece of foil and bake for a further 5-10 minutes or until it sounds hollow when tapped; do not overcook or it will be dry. Remove from the oven. Loosen the side of the tarte with a palette knife and then turn it out on to a clean tea-towel. Remove the paper. Wrap the tea-towel around the tarte and leave it to cool; this prevents it from forming a hard crust as it cools.

Make the crème pâtissière while the tarte is cooling: lightly beat together the eggs, sugar and flour. Bring the milk to the boil in a medium saucepan, then pour it on to the egg mixture, stirring continuously. Add the vanilla essence, then pour the mixture back into the pan and bring it slowly to the boil, stirring all the time. Remove from the heat and stir in the butter. Cover the surface of the crème pâtissière with damp greaseproof paper or cling film and leave to cool. Beat the double cream into the cold mixture.

Split the tarte in half horizontally and spread the crème pâtissière over the base. Place the other half on top and dust it generously with icing sugar.

GÂTEAU AU CHOCOLAT AVEC SAUCE VANILLE

CHOCOLATE CAKE WITH VANILLA SAUCE

This mouthwatering gâteau is served with its own vanilla sauce.

SERVES 8–10

CAKE

4 EGGS, SIZE 1, SEPARATED

175 G (6 OZ) CASTER SUGAR

5 ML (1 TSP) VANILLA ESSENCE

225 G (8 OZ) PLAIN CHOCOLATE

100 G (4 OZ) GROUND ALMONDS

75 G (3 OZ) PLAIN FLOUR

5 ML (1 TSP) BAKING POWDER

225 G (8 OZ) BUTTER

ICING SUGAR, FOR DREDGING

SAUCE

450 ML (¾ PINT) MILK

10 ML (2 TSP) VANILLA ESSENCE

4 EGG YOLKS

75 G (3 OZ) CASTER SUGAR

5 ML (1 TSP) CORNFLOUR OR POTATO FLOUR

Whisk the egg yolks with the sugar and vanilla essence in a bowl until smooth and creamy. Melt the chocolate in a bowl over a pan of hot water. Stir into the egg yolk mixture with the ground almonds, flour and baking powder. Melt the butter and, when only just warm, stir into the mixture. Whisk the egg whites until very stiff, then fold these in carefully. Transfer the mixture to the well buttered and base lined 26 cm (10¼ inch) flan dish.

Bake at 180°C (350°F) mark 4 for 30 minutes, then reduce the oven temperature to 160°C (325°F) mark 3 for a further 15 minutes, or until the cake is firm to the touch. Cool slightly, then turn out on to a wire rack. Dust with sifted icing sugar.

To make the sauce, heat the milk with the vanilla in a pan. Whisk the egg yolks, sugar and cornflour together in a basin. Pour on the hot milk, whisking all the time. Rinse the pan and return the sauce to it. Cook over a gentle heat, whisking continuously until smooth and thickened.

Serve the gâteau slightly warm, sliced, with a little of the sauce around it.

PARFAIT AUX NOIX FROID

CHILLED PARFAIT WITH NUTS

This recipe can be served on its own as a chilled cream dessert or served with fruit such as Oranges au caramel (see page 137).

SERVES 6

50 G (2 OZ) WALNUTS, FINELY CHOPPED

3 EGG YOLKS

1 WHOLE EGG

75 G (3 OZ) CASTER SUGAR

5 ML (1 TSP) VANILLA ESSENCE

15 ML (1 TBSP) BRANDY

300 ML (½ PINT) DOUBLE CREAM

Put the walnuts into a gratin dish and toast lightly and evenly under a hot grill. Cool. Put the eggs yolks, whole egg, sugar and vanilla into a basin over a pan of hot water. Whisk until thick and creamy. Cool, then stir in the brandy and nuts.

Whip the cream until thick, then carefully fold into the mixture. Divide into six individual serving dishes, such as ramekins, or one large shallow dish. Place in the freezer for 3–4 hours, or until just firm.

Overleaf: GÂTEAU AU CHOCOLAT AVEC SAUCE VANILLE

Preserves and Conserves

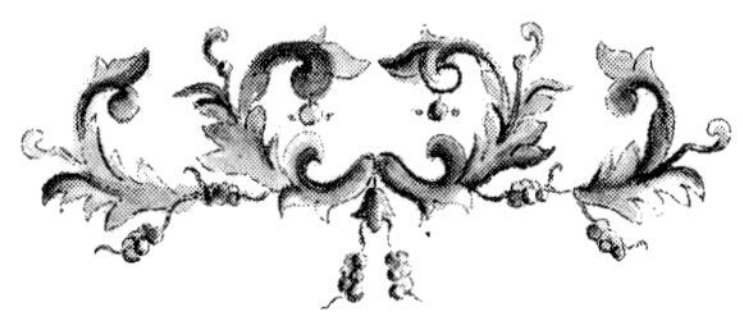

Testing for Setting

There are three tests for checking whether a preserve has reached setting point. If you have a sugar thermometer, lower it into the preserve to check the temperature: the preserve should set when it is boiling at about 110°C (230°F). Remember to heat the thermometer before putting it into the preserve and have a saucer ready for it afterwards.

The flake test is not as reliable as the temperature test. Lift a little preserve well above the pan on the spoon, then let it drop back into the pan quite slowly. If it begins to set in 'flakes' on the edge of the spoon, setting point is reached.

The saucer test is a good compromise between the above tests. Put a little preserve on a very cold saucer and leave it for about 2 minutes in a cool place. Push the preserve with your finger: if a distinct skin has formed and it wrinkles, then setting point is reached.

Preparing Jars for Preserves

Jam jars should be thoroughly washed in hot soapy water and rinsed in boiling water. They should be placed upside down on a folded clean tea-towel on a baking sheet. Put them in the oven at about 130°C (250°F) mark ½ for about 30 minutes, until they are hot and dry or until the preserve is ready for potting.

CONFITURE AUX ABRICOTS ET AUX AMANDES

APRICOT AND ALMOND JAM

The apricot kernels, together with the almonds, make this an interesting preserve.

MAKES 3.6 KG (8 LB)

1.8 G (4 LB) FRESH APRICOTS

GRATED RIND AND JUICE OF 3 LEMONS

1.4 KG (3 LB) PRESERVING SUGAR

100 G (4 OZ) BLANCHED ALMONDS, CHOPPED

Cut the apricots in half through to the stone, then twist the two halves to separate them and remove the stones. Crack open the stones with a hammer and take out the kernels. Place the kernels in a basin and cover with boiling water, leave for 1 minute, then drain them and remove their skins.

Place the apricots and the kernels in a large round cocotte or preserving pan. Pour in 600 ml (1 pint) water and add the lemon rind and juice. Heat gently until simmering, then simmer for 10–15 minutes or until the apricots are just soft.

Add the sugar and almonds to the pan. Heat gently, stirring all the time, until the sugar has dissolved. Bring the jam to the boil, then boil it rapidly until setting point is reached. See the note left on testing for setting. Use a spoon to skim the scum off the jam. Cool the preserve for about 10 minutes, then pour it into prepared jars. Cover at once with waxed discs, waxed-side down and airtight covers or lids. Label and store in a cool dark place.

CONFITURE AUX FIGUES ET AUX ORANGES

FIG AND ORANGE JAM

This jam is slightly unusual in that it is made with dried rather than fresh figs.

MAKES 1.8 KG (4 LB)

450 G (1 LB) DRIED FIGS

GRATED RIND AND JUICE OF 3 ORANGES

GRATED RIND AND JUICE OF 2 LEMONS

800 G (1¾ LB) PRESERVING SUGAR

Cut the figs in half and put them in a large round cocotte or preserving pan. Pour in 1.1 litres (2 pints) water. Add the orange and lemon rind and juice and leave the figs to soak overnight.

Next day, place the pan over a moderate heat and bring the fruit to the boil. Reduce the heat and simmer the fruit for about 1 hour or until the figs are very soft.

Add the sugar and heat gently, stirring all the time, until the sugar has dissolved. Bring the jam to the boil, then boil it rapidly until setting point is reached (see page 144). Skim all the scum off the jam, then allow it to cool for 10 minutes. Stir the jam, then pour it into prepared jars. Cover with waxed discs, waxed-side down, and airtight lids. Label the pots and store the jam in a cool dark place.

Overleaf: Left CONFITURE AUX FIGUES ET AUX ORANGES, *Centre* CONSERVE AUX FRAISES *(see page 149), Right* CONFITURE AUX ABRICOTS ET AUX AMANDES *(above)*

Pêches au Cognac

BRANDIED PEACHES

Other fruits, such as apricots and cherries (see below), can be preserved in this way.

MAKES ABOUT THREE 450 G (1 LB) JARS

900 G (2 LB) FRESH PEACHES

225 G (8 OZ) GRANULATED SUGAR

ABOUT 225 ML (8 FL OZ) BRANDY

To skin the peaches, plunge them into boiling water, then gently peel off the skins with your fingers. Halve the peaches and remove the stones.

Put 100 g (4 oz) of the sugar and 300 ml (½ pint) water in a saucepan and heat gently until the sugar has dissolved. Add the peaches to the syrup and poach gently for 4–5 minutes. Drain, reserving the syrup, and leave to cool for about 30 minutes.

Arrange the fruit in jars. Add the remaining sugar to the reserved syrup and dissolve it slowly. Bring to the boil and boil at 110°C (230°F) on a sugar thermometer. Cool for about 30 minutes.

Measure the syrup and add an equal quantity of brandy. Pour over the peaches. Cover at once with airtight tops, label and leave for at least 3 months.

Abricots au Cognac

BRANDIED APRICOTS

Use 900 g (2 lb) fresh apricots instead of the peaches.

Cerises au Cognac

BRANDIED CHERRIES

Use 450 g (1 lb) fresh cherries instead of the peaches. Prick the cherries all over with a darning needle, then poach in the syrup and continue as for peaches.

Liqueur d'Abricots

APRICOT LIQUEUR

This potent fruit liqueur uses dry white wine and gin.

MAKES ABOUT 1.4 LITRES (2½ PINTS)

450 G (1 LB) APRICOTS

450 G (1 LB) GRANULATED SUGAR

70 CL BOTTLE OF DRY WHITE WINE

300 ML (½ PINT) GIN

Wash the apricots, cut in half and remove the stones. Crack the stones and remove the kernels from inside. Blanch the kernels in boiling water for 1 minute.

Place the apricots, sugar and wine in a saucepan and heat gently, stirring, until the sugar has dissolved. Bring to the boil, then remove from the heat. Stir in the gin and apricot kernels. Pour into a large bowl or jug, cover tightly and leave for 5–6 days. Strain the liqueur through muslin, then bottle and label. Leave in a cool, dark place for at least 1 month before using.

Vinaigre aux Fraises ou Framboises

STRAWBERRY OR RASPBERRY VINEGAR

There is something extremely satisfying about making and using a home-made fruit vinegar. If you wish, you can make this vinegar sweeter by adding 175 g (6 oz) of sugar. Put the sugar into the pan with the vinegar, heat it until the sugar has dissolved, then boil for 1 minute. Remove from the heat and cool slightly before pouring into the bottles.

MAKES ABOUT 750 ML (1¼ PINTS)

450 G (1 LB) RASPBERRIES OR STRAWBERRIES

600 ML (1 PINT) WHITE WINE VINEGAR

SUGAR, OPTIONAL

Wash the fruit. Halve or quarter the strawberries. Place in a large bowl and crush lightly. Pour the vinegar over the fruit, cover with a cloth or piece of cling film and leave for 3–5 days, stirring from time to time.

Strain the liquid through a piece of muslin or a scalded tea-towel. Pour the fruit vinegar into sterilised bottles and cork (see note below). Leave to mature for at least 2 weeks before using. Use within 6 months.

Note: When sealing bottles with a cork, new corks should always be used and they should be soaked for 10 minutes in boiling water first in order to soften them. Once the bottles have been filled, they should be corked and the corks should be wired down to prevent them from blowing out. Alternatively the corks may be sealed in place with sealing wax.

Conserve aux Fraises

STRAWBERRY CONSERVE

In this conserve the fruit is suspended in a thick syrup which does not set firmly. It can be used as a filling for tarts or it may be spread on fresh bread.

MAKES ABOUT 2.7 KG (6 LB)

1.8 KG (4 LB) STRAWBERRIES

1.8 KG (4 LB) GRANULATED OR PRESERVING SUGAR

GRATED RIND AND JUICE OF 2 LEMONS

Layer the fruit and sugar in a bowl. Cover with a tea-towel or cling film and leave for 24 hours. This will extract all the juice from the fruit.

Strain the fruit and put all the syrup in a large round cocotte or preserving pan. Reserve the fruit. Add the lemon rind and juice to the pan. Heat gently, stirring, until all the sugar has dissolved, then bring the syrup to the boil. Boil the syrup rapidly until it is reduced by half, then add the fruit and cook for a further 5 minutes or until the fruit is tender. Do not over-cook the fruit or it will be mushy. Remove the pan from the heat and allow the preserve to cool completely. Ladle the preserve into sterilised jars, cover and label.

Overleaf: Left VINAIGRE AUX HERBES *(see page 154)*, VINAIGRE AUX FRAISES OU FRAMBOISES *(above)*

Framboise à l'Alcool

RASPBERRIES IN ALCOHOL

A delicious fruit based alcohol that forms the basis of champagne or sparkling wine aperitifs and cocktails.

MAKES 900 G (2 LB)

900 G (2 LB) RASPBERRIES

ALCOHOL, SUCH AS KIRSCH OR BRANDY

A LITTLE SUGAR

Wash the fruit, dry and remove the hulls. Pack the fruit into sterilised jars with tight fitting, non-metallic lids. Cover the fruit with the chosen alcohol and secure down the lids. Leave in a cool dark place for 1 month. Add 15–30 ml (1–2 tbsp) sugar to each jar, depending on desired sweetness, and stir in carefully. Replace the lids and store again for 1 month or longer. (The longer it is stored, the fuller the flavour.)

To serve, place 15 ml (1 tbsp) of the mixture into a glass and top up with champagne or sparkling wine.

Poires aux Epices

SPICED PEARS

Spiced with cinnamon, cloves and ginger, choose firm dessert pears for this unusual preserve.

MAKES 900 G (2 LB)

900 G (2 LB) FIRM EATING PEARS, PEELED, CORED AND QUARTERED

450 ML (¾ PINT) CIDER VINEGAR

450 G (1 LB) SUGAR

1 CINNAMON STICK

10 CLOVES

1 SMALL PIECE OF ROOT GINGER

Place the pears in a saucepan, cover with boiling water and cook gently for about 5 minutes until almost tender. Drain.

Pour the vinegar into a pan and add 300 ml (½ pint) water, the sugar, cinnamon, cloves and root ginger. Heat gently, stirring, until the sugar has dissolved, then boil for 5 minutes. Add the pears and continue cooking until the pears are tender.

Remove the pears with a slotted spoon and pack into preserving jars. Strain the vinegar syrup to remove the spices and pour over the pears to cover. Cover the jars immediately with airtight and vinegar-proof tops.

Prunes Confites

PICKLED PLUMS

The plums are pricked all over to absorb the flavour of the spiced mixture.

MAKES TWO
450 G (1 LB) JARS

450 G (1 LB) GRANULATED SUGAR

THINLY PARED RIND OF ½ LEMON

2 CLOVES

1 SMALL PIECE ROOT GINGER, PEELED AND BRUISED

300 ML (½ PINT) MALT VINEGAR

900 G (2 LB) PLUMS

Place all the ingredients, except the plums, in a large saucepan. Heat gently, stirring, until the sugar has dissolved, then bring to the boil. Remove from the heat and leave until cold.

Strain the spiced vinegar, return to the pan and bring to the boil again. Prick the plums and place in a deep bowl. Pour over the spiced vinegar. Cover and leave for 5 days. Strain the vinegar into a saucepan, bring to the boil and pour over the fruit again. Cover and leave for another 5 days.

Strain the vinegar into a pan and bring to the boil again. Pack the plums into two preserving jars and pour the boiling vinegar over. Cover the jars immediately with airtight and vinegar-proof tops.

Gelée aux Pommes et au Romarin

ROSEMARY APPLE JELLY

MAKES ABOUT SIX
450 G (1 LB) JARS

2.3 KG (5 LB) COOKING APPLES

30 ML (2 TBSP) FRESH ROSEMARY LEAVES

1.1 LITRES (2 PINTS) MALT VINEGAR

GRANULATED OR PRESERVING SUGAR

GREEN FOOD COLOURING

SPRIGS OF FRESH ROSEMARY

Remove any bruised or damaged portions from the apples and chop them roughly into thick chunks without peeling or coring. Put the apples in a large cocotte or preserving pan with 1.1 litres (2 pints) water and the rosemary. Bring to the boil, then simmer for about 45 minutes until soft and pulpy. Stir from time to time to prevent sticking. Add the vinegar and boil for a further 5 minutes. Spoon the apple pulp into a jelly bag or cloth attached to the legs of an upturned stool. Allow the juice to strain into a large bowl for at least 12 hours. Do not squeeze the bag or the jelly will be cloudy. Discard the pulp. Measure the extract and return to the pan with 450 g (1 lb) sugar to every 600 ml (1 pint) extract. Stir until the sugar has dissolved. Bring to the boil and boil rapidly, without stirring, for about 10 minutes until setting point is reached, when a temperature of 105°C (221°F) is reached on a sugar thermometer. (See note on page 144.) Remove the pan from the heat. Skim the surface with a slotted spoon to remove any scum. Add a few drops of colouring and stir. Pour into warmed jars and add a sprig of rosemary to each. Place a disc of waxed paper across the surface of the jelly, then cover and label the jar. Store in a cool, dry, dark place for up to 1 year.

Chanterelles au Vinaigre

PICKLED MUSHROOMS

When selecting the mushrooms for this pickle, make sure they are firm textured with fresh looking stalks – not brown and withered.

MAKES 450 G (1 LB)

450 G (1 LB) CHANTERELLES OR OTHER FIRM MUSHROOMS

30 ML (2 TBSP) COOKING SALT

4 SHALLOTS, SKINNED AND THINLY SLICED

5 ML (1 TSP) BLACK PEPPERCORNS

FEW THYME SPRIGS

1 BAY LEAF

450 ML (¾ PINT) WHITE VINEGAR

5 ML (1 TSP) SUGAR

Place the mushrooms in a cocotte and sprinkle over the salt. Cover and leave overnight. Strain off the juices from the mushrooms and cover with freshly boiled water. Leave for 5 minutes, then strain and discard the water.

Put the mushrooms, shallots, peppercorns, thyme and bay leaf into a preserving jar. Boil the vinegar and add the sugar. Immediately pour over the mushrooms, making sure that they are completely covered. Seal the jar and store for several weeks before using.

Vinaigre aux Herbes

HERB VINEGAR

Tarragon is the most usual herb used to flavour vinegar; however other herbs may be used, including dill, marjoram, mint, sage and basil.

MAKES 600 ML (1 PINT)

100–175 G (4–6 OZ) FRESH HERBS

600 ML (1 PINT) WHITE WINE VINEGAR

1 EXTRA HERB SPRIG

Wash and dry the herbs thoroughly. Put the leaves in a large jar and bruise them with the end of a rolling pin or a wooden spoon. Pour the vinegar over the herbs, cover the bowl and leave it in a cool, dark place for 3 weeks. Place a fresh sprig of the relevant herb in a bottle. Strain the vinegar through a piece of muslin, then pour it into the bottle. Cork the bottle and leave the vinegar to mature for 2 weeks before using.

Basic Recipes

Fond Brun

BEEF BONE STOCK

This is a good basic stock recipe which can be adapted to suit your needs and whatever is available. Stock freezes well, but to save space in the freezer, you may prefer to reduce it by about three-quarters, then freeze it in the form of ice cubes, which, when defrosted can be reconstituted to their original strength.

MAKES 1.7 LITRES (3 PINTS)

- 900 G (2 LB) BEEF BONES, TRIMMED OF EXCESS FAT, CHOPPED INTO PIECES
- 100 G (4 OZ) SHIN OF BEEF
- 1 ONION, SKINNED AND ROUGHLY CHOPPED
- 1 CARROT, PEELED AND ROUGHLY CHOPPED
- 1 SMALL TURNIP, PEELED AND ROUGHLY CHOPPED
- 1 LEEK, TRIMMED AND SLICED
- 2 CELERY STICKS, SLICED
- 1 BOUQUET GARNI
- A FEW BLACK PEPPERCORNS
- SALT

Wash the bones well. Put the bones and shin of beef, if using, into a large round cocotte. Pour in 3.4 litres (6 pints) cold water. Bring slowly to simmering point, then simmer, uncovered, for about 15 minutes, skimming off all the grey scum that rises to the surface. Add all the vegetables, the bouquet garni and peppercorns. Cover and simmer very gently for 4–5 hours. During cooking, occasionally skim off any fat and scum which comes to the surface. Allow the stock to cool, then strain it and add salt to taste. Leave the stock until quite cold then lift off any fat that sets on the surface.

Fond Blanc

VEAL STOCK OR WHITE STOCK

Make as for brown stock above, using veal bones instead of beef bones. Substitute stewing veal for the shin of beef and omit the turnip.

Fond de Volaille ou de Gibier

POULTRY OR GAME STOCK

Make as the beef bone stock on page 155, but replace the beef bones and beef with the carcass of chicken, duck, hare, pheasant or other poultry or game. Add the giblets but omit the turnip and reduce the quantity of water to 1.1 litres (2 pints). Uncooked bones give a better stock and they should be simmered for about 2 hours. Bones which have already been cooked (for example, left from a roast) should be simmered for only 45 minutes.

Pâte Brisée

SHORT CRUST PASTRY

Throughout the recipes, the following is referred to as '1 quantity'.

MAKES 225 G (8 OZ)

225 G (8 OZ) PLAIN FLOUR
PINCH OF SALT
100 G (4 OZ) BUTTER
1 EGG

Sift the flour and salt on to a clean work surface. Cut the butter up into small cubes. Make a well in the centre of the flour and put the butter in it. Add the egg. Using your fingertips, work the butter and egg together with the flour until it is well blended. The dough should cling together leaving the work surface clean: if it is too dry add a few *drops* of water. Knead the dough lightly for about 3 minutes, until it forms a smooth ball, then put it into a polythene bag and chill for at least 30 minutes before using. Use as required.

Crêpes

PANCAKES

This is a basic batter which may be used for both sweet and savoury pancakes.

MAKES ABOUT 6 LARGE PANCAKES OR 8 SMALL ONES

25 G (1 OZ) BUTTER
100 G (4 OZ) PLAIN FLOUR
2.5 ML (½ TSP) SALT (OPTIONAL: SEE METHOD)
2 EGGS
300 ML (½ PINT) MILK
OIL FOR FRYING

Melt the butter and leave it to cool. Sift the flour into a bowl. If unsalted butter is used, then add the salt. Make a well in the flour and add the eggs, then gradually beat in the milk and butter incorporating the eggs and flour, to make a smooth batter.

Pour a little oil into the base of a crêpe pan and put it on the heat until it is hot. Quickly pour in enough batter to cover the base of the pan thinly, tilting the pan to cover it evenly. Cook until the underside of the pancake is golden brown, then turn or toss the pancake and cook on the second side until it is golden. Pile the cooked pancakes on a plate, separating each one with a piece of non-stick baking parchment or greaseproof paper.

LE CREUSET RANGE

FRYING, OMELETTE PANS AND SKILLETS

Non-Stick Frying Pan *Wooden handle*

2016.23 9"/23cm
2016.26 10 1/4"/26cm
2016.29 11 1/4"/29cm

Non-Stick Omelette Pan *Iron handle*

2036.20 8"/20cm
2036.24 9 1/2"/24cm

Non-Stick Skillet *Iron handle*

2051.16 6 1/4"/16cm
2051.23 9"/23cm
2051.26 10 1/4"/26cm

SAUCEPANS

Non-Stick Milk Pan *Wooden handle*

2005.16 2pt/1.1L

Saucepan *Wooden handle*

2539.14 1 1/4pt/0.7L
2539.16 2pt/1.1L
2539.18 2 2/3pt/1.5L
2539.20 3 1/3pt/1.9L
2539.22 4 3/4pt/2.7L

Iron handle

2507.16 2pt/1.1L
2507.18 2 2/3pt/1.5L
2507.20 3 1/3pt/1.9L
2507.22 4 3/4pt/2.7L

Non-Stick Marmitout *Multi-Function Iron handle*

2531.18 1 3/4pt/1.0L
2531.22 3pt/1.8L
2531.26 5 1/4pt/3.0L

COCOTTES, CASSEROLES

Round Cocotte

2501.18 3 1/3pt/1.9L
2501.20 4 1/2pt/2.6L
2501.22 6pt/3.4L
2501.24 7 1/2pt/4.3L
2501.26 9 1/2pt/5.5L
2501.28 12pt/6.8L
2501.30 14 3/4pt/8.4L
2501.34 21 1/2pt/12.3L

Oval Cocotte

2502.25 5 3/4pt/3.3L
2502.27 7 1/4pt/4.2L
2502.29 8 1/4pt/4.8L
2502.30 9 1/4pt/5.3L
2502.31 11 1/4pt/6.5L
2502.35 15 3/4pt/9.0L

Round Casserole

2515.14 3/4pt/0.5L
2515.18 1 3/4pt/1.0L
2515.22 3pt/1.8L

Shallow Round Casserole

2503.24 4 1/3pt/2.5L

Oval Casserole

2506.22 3pt/1.7L
2506.26 4 1/3pt/2.5L

Buffet Casserole

2532.26 3 3/4pt/2.2L
2532.30 6pt/3.4L

GRATINS, OVEN DISHES

Oval Gratin

0013.20 8"/20cm
0013.24 9 1/2"/24cm
0013.28 11"/28cm
0013.32 12 1/2"/32cm
0013.36 14 1/4"/36cm

Round Gratin

2010.15 6"/15cm
2010.18 7"/18cm
2010.22 8 3/4"/22cm

Rectangular Oven Dish

2011.30 11 3/4"x8"/ 30 x 20cm
2011.40 15 3/4"x10"/ 40 x 25cm

Egg Plate

2009.03 6 1/4"/16cm

Snail Plate

0017.06 5 1/2"/14cm

Pâté Terrine

2524.28 2pt/1.1L
2524.32 2 2/3pt/1.5L

LE CREUSET SETS

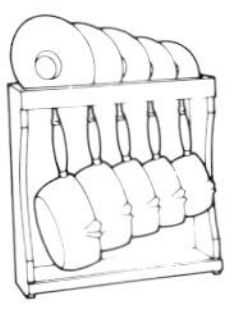

2439 • 5 Wooden handled Saucepans 14,16,18,20 &22cm, plus Pine Rack

2433 • 3 Wooden handled Saucepans 16,18 & 20cm plus Pine Rack

2540 • 3 Wooden handled Saucepans 16,18 & 20cm, Non-Stick Milk Pan, Non- Stick Frying Pan, plus Pine Rack

FONDUE SETS

6001 • Iron handled, Dual-function, 6 forks, alcohol heater

6034 • Phenolic handled, Dual-function 6 forks, alcohol heater

6071 • Dual-function, 6 forks, alcohol heater, Enamelled Cast Iron stand

3610 • Cheese, 6 forks, alcohol heater

6800 • Chocolate, 4 forks candle heater

GRILLS, CREPE PANS

Round Grill 2048 9" dia./23cm

Meat Grill 2049 14x8"/36 x 20cm

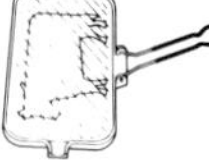

Giant Grill 0053 18x9"/46 x 23cm

Grillomat 2054 91/2 x 91/2"/24x24cm

Breton Crepe Pan 7049.4 10 3/4"/27cm dia.

Normandy Crepe Pan 7050.3 9 1/2" /24cm dia.
7050.4 10 3/4" /27cm dia.

Soufflé Dish 0069.22 5pt/2.9L

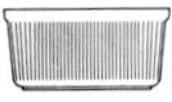

Flan Dish 0067.26 10" /25cm dia.

STEAMERS

Enamelled Steel. Fits equivalent sized Traditional Cocotte

4020.18 7 1/4"/18cm
4020.22 8 3/4"/22cm
4020.24 9 1/2"/24cm

DURAMEL RANGE

Frying Pan

Wooden handle
2408.28 11"/28cm

Skillet

Iron handle
2451.23 9"/23cm
2451.26 10 1/4"/26cm

Cassadou

Iron handle
2456.23 4pt/2.3L
2456.27 6 1/2pt/3.7L

VITROBASE RANGE

Non-Stick Frying Pan 7068.26 10 1/4"/26cm

Non-Stick Milk Pan 7066.16 1 3/4pt/1.0L

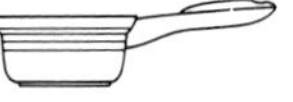

Saucepan with Lids
7566.14 1pt/0.6L
7566.16 1 3/4pt/1.0L
7566.18 2 1/4pt/1.3L
7566.20 3 1/3pt/1.9L
7566.22 5pt/2.9L

Oval Gratin Dish
7065.27 10 1/2"/27cm
7065.29 11 1/4"/29cm

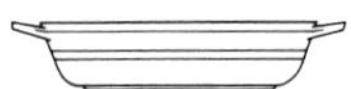

Round Casserole
7563.21 4 1/2pt/2.6L
7563.23 5 1/2pt/3.1L
7563.26 7 1/2pt/4.3L
7563.29 11pt/6.3L

Oval Casserole
7564.27 6pt/3.4L
7564.29 7 1/2pt/4.3L
5764.33 11pt/6.3L

FREE HELPLINE. IF YOU HAVE ANY QUESTIONS ABOUT LE CREUSET (BEFORE OR AFTER YOU BUY) CALL LE CREUSET FREE - WE WILL BE DELIGHTED TO HELP. DIAL **0800-37-37-92** (MONDAY TO FRIDAY 10am-4 pm) UK ONLY.

10 YEAR GUARANTEE. ALL LE CREUSET PRODUCTS ARE GUARANTEED FOR TEN YEARS AGAINST FAILURES CAUSED BY FAULTY MATERIALS OR WORKMANSHIP. THIS GUARANTEE DOES NOT AFFECT YOUR STATUTORY RIGHTS AND IS VALID FOR TEN YEARS.

NB. SOME COLOUR PHOTOGRAPHS USED IN THIS BOOK INCLUDE LE CREUSET SHAPES WHICH ARE NOT CURRENTLY AVAILABLE IN THE U.K.

INDEX